# Microwaving
# for
# 1 or 2

# Microwaving for 1 or 2

## 200 Innovative Recipes Using Fresh Ingredients

Susan Brown Draudt

G.K.HALL &CO.
Boston, Massachusetts
1990

Published in Large Print by arrangement with
HPBooks, a division of
Price, Stern, Sloan Incorporated.

G. K. Hall Large Print Book Series.

Set in 18 pt. Plantin.

**Library of Congress Cataloging-in-Publication Data**

Draudt, Susan Brown.
   Microwaving for 1 or 2 : 200 innovative recipes using fresh
ingredients / Susan Brown Draudt.
      p.    cm. — (G.K. Hall large print book series)
   ISBN 0-8161-5030-3 (hc). — ISBN 0-8161-5031-1 (pb)
   1. Microwave cookery.  2. Cookery for one.  3. Cookery for two.
4. Large type books.  I. Title.  II. Title: Microwaving for one or
two.
[TX832.D73  1990]
641.5′882—dc20                             90-37602

# Contents

# Microwaving
## for
## 1 or 2

# Introduction

Do you find yourself saying "I don't want to take the time to cook for just myself." Or "with both of us working there isn't time to prepare a great meal during the week." Or could it be "most recipes are for four to six servings; there's always so much left over." If you answered "yes" to any of these questions, *Microwave Cooking for 1 or 2* is just the book you need. Microwave ovens are the greatest timesavers. Combining your oven and these recipes geared to one or two persons, there's no excuse not to create interesting and quick meals.

From teaching microwave cooking classes, I have found the majority of microwave oven owners want to use their appliances much more than they do. This book should be the stimulus you need to get better educated and excited about using your microwave oven. It highlights the areas in which I feel a microwave oven makes meal preparation faster, tastier and all-around more fun.

Everyone wants to spend less time in the kitchen but, at the same time, create recipes that look and taste like they slaved all day. Each chapter is filled with recipes that will

1

quickly become favorite standbys because you almost always have the basic ingredients on hand. There are also some spectacularly impressive recipes that will really make you wonder how you survived without a microwave oven.

In microwave cooking, learning a few basic procedures is the key to success. Start reading this book right at the beginning whether you're a novice or a pro. The introduction is a real "how-to" chapter. It will show you the best ways to utilize your microwave oven for great results every time. Chapters span from appetizers to desserts and everything in between. This book is a guide for the small household microwave oven user and contains the most important information on the appliance itself: what it will and will not do, proper utensils and techniques, preparation of food and recipes you will need. Most of all, this book is filled with creative recipes you will want to prepare time and time again.

I have found most microwave oven owners have two things in common. First, they lack the confidence to try cooking new recipes. This is understandable because microwaving is a whole new ball game and they need to know a few basic rules and techniques to get them started. Second, they overcook food once they do venture out. Microwave ovens cook food in seconds, not minutes. To heat a roll takes only five seconds, hardly enough time to turn the microwave oven on, then off. Begin by cooking everything much, much less than you could ever imagine. It's easy to add five or ten seconds of cooking time if the food is not quite done.

A microwave oven can handle nearly everything you cook on top of a conventional range except frying and heating sugar to a high temperature for candy-making. You'll also be able to microwave most of what you do in a conventional oven with the exception of giving a crunchy crust to a bread or pastry product or baking a soufflé or a meringue.

If you are confused by all the different temperature/cooking settings, start by using 100% (HIGH). About 80% of all microwaving can be done on 100% (HIGH). Lower power settings are used for protein dishes like eggs, cheese and some meats. By lowering the power level you are lessening the amount of microwave energy. The magnatron tube will cycle on and off at different intervals instead of constantly emitting microwave energy. This way you can slow your cooking down. If you have an early model with only one power level, which is 100%

(HIGH), you can slow down the cooking process by manually turning the microwave oven on and off if the food seems to be cooking too quickly.

The recipes in this book were tested using several variable power microwave ovens between 600 and 700 watts.

*Terms*

Becoming familiar with these terms will help you master your microwave oven.

**Cover loosely**—Use wax paper, a paper towel or a casserole lid slightly ajar to allow some moisture to escape and to reduce spattering.

**Cover tightly**—Use a casserole lid, vented plastic wrap or a plate to keep in moisture and steam, thus speeding up cooking time and eliminating spattering.

To vent plastic wrap, turn back one corner or poke four to five knife holes in the top of tight plastic wrap.

**Elevate**—Set foods like quiche or quick bread batter on top of an inverted dinner plate or rack so the bottom can easily absorb microwaves to insure even cooking.

**Standing time**—Dense foods such as meats, casseroles and some vegetables require extra time after microwaving to complete cooking or to evenly disperse heat. Usually the foods are wrapped or covered during microwaving or, as in the case of potatoes, wrapped in foil or covered with a bowl immediately after microwaving to retain heat.

**Rotate**—Move food to a different place in a microwave oven or turn over to give a more evenly cooked product.

**Pierce**—Foods with a thick skin or membrane (like potatoes, acorn squash or egg yolks) need to be pierced. This lets steam easily escape so foods won't pop and explode. Use the tines of a fork, a sharp knife or a wooden pick.

*Cookware*

**Handy Basic Utensils**
  Custard cups
  Glass measures—1-, 2- and 4-cup sizes
  Casserole dishes—15- and 20-ounce sizes
  Pie plates—4½- and 7-inch sizes
  Quiche dish—10-ounce size
  Browning dish

**Paper**—Towels, plates and cups.

**Baskets**—Unvarnished wicker baskets without staples can be used for very short cooking times like heating a sandwich or reheating rolls.

**Plastic**—Check label for microwave use. Plastic utensils vary in the amount of heat they can take. Most can be used for microwaving water-based foods (drinks, vegetables). Microwaving fatty foods in plastic is not recommended as the fat gets very hot very fast and can blister or warp the plastic.

**Plastic microwave cookware**—There is a large variety on the market. Read labels to see if high-fat or high-sugar foods can be cooked in them. As a clue, if a manufacturer says top-rack dishwasher-safe only, generally the plastic will not withstand foods that reach high temperatures.

**Plastic cooking bags**—Be sure to close with a strip of plastic or a rubber band, never a metal tie. Pierce two or three steam-vent holes in the top. Do not use plastic produce bags as they will melt.

**Metal**—Metal utensils are not recommended. Check your manufacturer's directions in the use and care booklet which came with your microwave oven. Aluminum foil dishes (like the type TV dinners come in) should be at least three-fourths full of food. Never allow metal to touch the sides of a microwave oven; this could damage the appliance.

**Food packages & jars**—Vegetables can be cooked in their cardboard packages. Set the package on a plate so any liquid will not spill. Reheat syrup, jam or spaghetti sauce in their own glass jars with lids removed to allow for steam escape. Remember, the jar will probably be hot.

Check your cupboards for glass or micro-wave-safe utensils you already have like bowls, plates and casserole dishes. If a dish has gold or silver trim, do not use it for microwaving as the trim may darken or overheat the area next to the trim and crack the dish.

To test a dish for safe microwave use, fill a glass measure with ½ cup cold water. Set it in the microwave oven beside the dish you want to test. Microwave on 100% (HIGH) one minute. If the dish remains cool, it can be used for microwave cooking. If warm or hot, the dish should not be used for micro-wave cooking.

*Coverings*

Coverings are used to keep moisture in, to prevent liquid foods from spattering and to heat food more evenly and quickly. There are four types of covers commonly used.

1. **Lids**—May be used to cover glass, ceramic or plastic cookware. Or use a microwave-safe dinner plate as a covering. What a terrific way to warm your dinner plates before serving (heat is transferred from the food to the plate).
2. **Plastic wrap**—Best for steaming vegetables or reheating foods to keep in as much moisture as possible.
3. **Wax paper**—Traps some steam for more even heat distribution yet allows browning to occur on longer-cooking foods such as beef, poultry and pork. It is also recommended for casseroles. Wax paper won't melt in a microwave oven.
4. **Paper towels**—Ideal for covering foods that may spatter, such as bacon, and for absorbing excess moisture from bread products.

*Defrosting*

The defrost cycle on a microwave oven is about a 30% (MEDIUM-LOW) to 50% (MEDIUM) on-off cycle. Microwaves first heat up the outside of any food and the heat is transferred inward. The "off," or standing time, during defrosting gives the temperature of the food time to equalize throughout so the outer edges are not overcooked while the center is still frozen. If your microwave oven has only one speed, you can defrost food but you must turn the oven on and off manually.

Small portions of food like breads, pastries and frozen vegetables defrost quickly with little attention. Larger more dense types of food like meat, poultry and fish defrost slowly with a greater chance of overcooking the outside before the center is defrosted. These types of food need to be turned over or rotated once or twice while defrosting.

Consult your manufacturer's use and care booklet for correct defrosting instructions for your microwave oven.

With a microwave, leftovers are a plus! Reheating foods, especially for one or two people, is made easier and foods are more flavorful with a microwave oven. Foods taste fresh, not reheated. Reheating also comes in handy for pastries in the morning or giving a slice of pie that just-baked aroma and flavor. Cold dinner rolls are a thing of the past; remember one roll may take only five seconds to reheat. Always use the least amount of time given for reheating. With refrigerated foods, the dish may feel cool when the food inside has reached serving temperature.

When reheating most foods, with the exception of breads and pastries, cover tightly to prevent moisture loss through evaporation. Rolls and bread products like pizza should be set on a paper towel to absorb moisture and prevent the food from becoming soggy. It's best to let some foods stand two to three minutes after reheating to let heat distribute evenly.

To reheat foods listed below, microwave on 70% (MEDIUM-HIGH).

|  | Amount | Microwaving Time | Standing Time |
|---|---|---|---|
| Rolls | 2 | 10 to 15 seconds | 0 |
| Pastry | 1 | 10 to 15 seconds | 0 |
| **Meat** | | | |
| Chop | 1 (6-oz.) | 1 to 1½ minutes | 1 minute |
| Sliced Meat | 8 oz. | 2 to 3 minutes | 1 minute |
| Casseroles | 1 cup | 1 to 2 minutes | 3 minutes |
| Plate of Foods | 1 | 1½ to 2½ minutes | 3 minutes |
| **Sandwiches** | | | |
| Open-Faced | 1 | 1 to 1½ minutes | 0 |
| Closed | 1 | 1 to 1½ minutes | 1 minute |
| Pie | 1 slice | 1 minute | 1 minute |

## *Increasing/Decreasing a Microwave Recipe*

Microwave cooking time is affected by the amount and depth of food.

**To double a microwave recipe**—Use twice the amount of solid ingredients and one and three-fourths the amount of liquid. Cooking time will need to be increased one-half to

11

three-fourths of original time. Check food carefully during cooking; additional liquid may need to be added.

**To halve a recipe**—Use one-half the amount of all ingredients (dry and liquid) and decrease cooking time by one-half to two-thirds of original time.

These cooking times are approximate, so check food often.

*Converting Conventional Recipes*

1. Find a similar microwave recipe and start with the same amount of solid ingredients.
2. Reduce the amount of liquid in the conventional recipe by one-fourth. You can always add more, if necessary, later.
3. Use slightly less seasoning to begin with; shorter cooking time often enhances flavor.
4. Adding fat, such as cooking oil, to grease the pan can be eliminated. This fat attracts energy and slows cooking.
5. Follow a similar microwave recipe for appropriate dish size, covering instructions and cooking time.

6. If you do not have a similar recipe to follow for cooking time, start by reducing microwave cooking time to one-fourth of conventional cooking time. Check food often.
7. Always undercook food as it can quickly become dry. More cooking time can always be added, if necessary.

When using this book, remember:

1. All cooking utensils must be microwave-safe—glass, plastic, ceramic or paper.
2. Cooking power is specified in each recipe.
3. It's always a good idea to stir or rotate foods that are microwaved longer than two minutes.
4. To tightly cover foods when microwaving, use plastic wrap or a tight-fitting lid if you want to keep in moisture. Cover with wax paper or a paper towel if you want to let some moisture escape or to keep spattering down. Do not cover at all if you want some moisture to evaporate such as when making a sauce or microwaving a potato.
5. To prevent large amounts of steam from building up when covering dishes with plastic wrap, fold back one corner of the

wrap. This makes a small vent which reduces the possibility of burns when removing the wrap.

6. Plastic wrap should be microwave-suitable. The box will state if safe for microwave use. The thinner wraps will sometimes melt from the high temperatures of food.

## Storage & Special Handling of Staple Food Items

In a one- or two-person household, I have found staple food items often take a while to be used. I find it helpful to mark the purchase date on containers of herbs, spices and baking soda. Most brands of baking powder have an expiration date marked on the bottom. Below is a chart for staple food items regarding storage time and special handling.

| Food | Time | Special Handling |
|------|------|------------------|
| Baking powder | 18 months | Keep covered and dry. |
| Bread crumbs, dried | 6 months | Keep covered and dry. |
| Flour (all types) | 1 year | Store in airtight container. |

| Food | Time | Special Handling |
|---|---|---|
| Honey, jam and syrup | 1 year | Keep tightly covered. If sugar crystalizes, microwave to dissolve. |
| Nonfat dry milk | 1 year | Keep cool and dry. |
| Sugar | | |
| brown | 4 months | Store in airtight container. |
| powdered | 1 year | Store in airtight container. |
| granulated | 2 years | Store in airtight container. |
| Vegetables, canned or dried | 1 year | Keep cool. |
| Herbs and spices | | |
| whole spices | 1 year | Transfer to airtight containers. |
| ground spices | 6 months | Keep away from heat and sunlight. |
| herbs | 6 months | Check aroma and color. If faded, replace. |

*Helpful Hints for the Chef*

Microwave tortilla chips on 100% (HIGH) 20 to 30 seconds just before serving for that freshly-made flavor.

To peel tomatoes or peaches, in a 2-cup glass measure, microwave 1 cup water on 100% (HIGH) 3 minutes or until boiling. Drop tomato or peach in water. Let stand 20 seconds. Remove with spoon. Rinse with cold water; peel.

To soften refrigerated peanut butter, microwave ¼ cup on 100% (HIGH) 30 seconds or until easy to stir.

To soften butter or margarine, unwrap and place in a custard cup. Microwave on 50% (MEDIUM): 2 tablespoons, 20 seconds; ¼ cup, 30 seconds. Watch closely!

To melt butter or margarine, unwrap and place in a custard cup. Microwave on 100% (HIGH): 2 tablespoons, 20 seconds; ¼ cup, 40 seconds.

To blanch almonds, in a 2-cup glass measure, microwave 1 cup water on 100% (HIGH) 3 minutes or until boiling. Remove from oven. Add ½ cup almonds. Let stand 5 minutes. Drain; rinse with cold water. Pinch almond to slip off skin.

To flame liqueur, in a 1-cup glass measure, microwave 2 tablespoons liqueur (80 proof or higher) on 100% (HIGH) 20 seconds. Pour on food and light.

To melt caramels, unwrap and place in a medium-size microwave-safe glass bowl. Microwave on 100% (HIGH) until melted: ½ cup (about 15), 1 minute; 1 cup (about 30), 1½ minutes. Stir once.

Let cake batter stand 5 minutes before microwaving to reduce unevenness on top. Fill pan only half full. Microwaved cakes rise higher than ones baked in a conventional oven.

To heat ice cream sauce, in a 1-cup glass measure, microwave ¼ cup on 100% (HIGH) 30 seconds or until hot; stir. These toppings are usually high in sugar and heat very quickly.

To soften ice cream, place a 1-pint carton in microwave oven. Microwave on 100% (HIGH) 15 seconds. Check for "spoonability." If needed, microwave on 100% (HIGH) 5 seconds more.

# APPETIZERS &
# BEVERAGES

Appetizers have never been more popular! Whether called hors d'oeuvres, tapas or pupus, everyone is always pleased to sample a few. Restaurants now feature full appetizer menus where an assortment of appetizers can be ordered to make a complete meal. The perfect meal for me is an assortment of appetizers and desserts. I need nothing else, except perhaps a glass of champagne, to complement both.

Microwave ovens and recipes geared to one or two servings are a perfect combination for easy and quick appetizers. As only small amounts of ingredients are necessary, splurge on shrimp, caviar or whatever suits your fancy. With emphasis on lighter, smaller meals, two or three appetizers can be a perfect dinner solution.

Try Bacon-Wrapped Watermelon Pickles. Sound a little strange? Everyone seems to like them, and wooden picks do not burn in a microwave oven.

Hot or warm appetizers are quickly cooked or reheated in a microwave oven without losing original fresh color or flavor. And if all are not eaten immediately, like Layered Brie where warmth brings out the best flavor, just reheat a few seconds.

And to go along with appetizers, an assortment of beverage recipes are in this chapter. Heated right in a microwave-safe mug, nothing beats hot cocoa or cider to warm wintry days and nights. Especially nice is not having to wash a dirty pan when through. If the mug or glass you want to use is not microwave-safe or you want to make extra servings, use a two- or four-cup glass measure or a microwave-safe teapot.

Any leftover beverage can be covered, refrigerated and quickly reheated in a microwave oven. The amount of time needed to reheat depends on the amount and temperature. Generally, you can reheat a beverage in a serving mug, microwave-safe teapot or coffee pot or a glass measure on 100% (HIGH) one to two minutes per serving. Stir after microwaving to evenly distribute heat. Leftover brewed coffee is great reheated later in the day. Be sure to remove the fresh pot from the heat as soon as it finishes brewing so the liquid will not continue to evaporate. This makes stronger coffee than the original. I know people who swear their microwave oven is the best tea kettle ever invented for boiling water—no more burned tea kettles. Instant coffee is really instant when one cup of water is brought to a boil in two to three minutes right in a serving mug. Tea is a delight done the same way.

Although hot drinks immediately come to mind when you think of a microwave oven, it also helps in the preparation of chilled drinks. For example, a microwave quickly heats water to dissolve sugar making a perfectly flavored Lemonade Syrup. Refrigerate and make a refreshing glass of lemonade later with no fuss. A microwave oven comes to the rescue in making a Brandy Slush. Defrost frozen concentrated juice by removing the metal top and placing the cardboard container (it's okay to leave on the metal bottom) in a microwave oven. Microwave on 100% (HIGH) forty-five seconds to one minute. The juice will not be completely defrosted, but can be easily poured into a pitcher. Iced tea begins with hot tea; brew your favorite tea double strength in a microwave oven. Pour into an ice cube-filled glass, ready to serve and refresh.

# Toasted Almond Camembert

Serve with grapes and French bread or crackers.

**1 teaspoon butter or margarine**
**1 tablespoon sliced almonds**
**1 (4½-oz.) Camembert cheese round**

In a small microwave-safe plate, microwave butter or margarine and almonds on 100% (HIGH) 1 minute. Remove from oven. Stir to coat. Place Camembert on top of almonds. Microwave on 100% (HIGH) 2 to 2½ minutes or until cheese is slightly melted around edges. Invert on a serving plate. Makes 2 servings.

# Layered Brie

Serve with Melba toast and apple slices, if desired.

**1 (4½-oz.) Brie cheese round, cut in**
**half crosswise**
**1 tablespoon crumbled blue cheese**
**1 tablespoon chopped pecans**

Place bottom half of cheese on a microwave-safe serving dish. Sprinkle with blue cheese and pecans. Place top half of cheese on bottom half. Microwave on 70% (MEDIUM-HIGH) 1 to 1½ minutes or until cheese is warm on sides. Makes 2 servings.

# Nachos

Prepare two plates as Nachos go fast! Serve one while microwaving another for a quick refill.

**2 cups taco-flavored tortilla chips**
**1 cup (4-oz.) shredded Cheddar or**
**Monterey Jack cheese**
**½ (4-oz.) can chopped green chilies**

Arrange ½ of chips in a single layer on a microwave-safe plate. Sprinkle with ½ of cheese. Top with ½ of green chilies. Microwave on 100% (HIGH) 30 seconds to 1 minute or until cheese is melted. Repeat procedure with remaining ingredients. Makes 2 servings.

**Variation**
Spoon ¼ (3½-oz.) can bean dip on 1 cup taco-flavored tortilla chips. Top with ½ cup

shredded Cheddar or Montery Jack cheese. Microwave on 100% (HIGH) 30 seconds to 1 minute or until cheese melts. Repeat procedure for another serving.

# Vegetable Bundles

Green onion stems are used to tie these bundles.

**8 (2-inch) julienne strips carrot**
**8 (2-inch) julienne strips red bell pepper**
**8 (2-inch) julienne strips zucchini**
**4 (8-inch) green onion stems**
**1 tablespoon Italian salad dressing**
**4 (3- × 1-inch) thin slices Monterey Jack cheese**

In a small microwave-safe dish, place carrot strips, bell pepper, zucchini and green onion stems. Cover tightly. Microwave on 100% (HIGH) 30 seconds. Pour Italian dressing over vegetables. Stir to coat; re-cover. Refrigerate until chilled. To assemble, place 2 strips each of carrot, bell pepper and zucchini crosswise on 1 end of each piece of cheese. Roll up cheese. Tie 1 green onion stem around middle of each bundle. Makes 2 servings.

# Chutney Potato Skins

A delicious contrast of warm, cool and spicy!

**2 (5-oz.) baking potatoes, pierced**
**¼ teaspoon curry powder**
**⅓ cup dairy sour cream**
**2 tablespoons chutney, chopped**
**¼ cup (1-oz.) shredded Cheddar cheese**

Place potatoes in microwave oven. Microwave on 100% (HIGH) 3 minutes. Turn potatoes over. Microwave on 100% (HIGH) 3 to 5 minutes more or until potatoes give slightly when squeezed. Wrap in foil or place under an inverted mixing bowl 20 minutes or until cool. Cut each potato in half lengthwise. Scoop out pulp, leaving a ¼-inch shell.

Reserve pulp for another use. Place potato skins on a microwave-safe serving plate. Sprinkle inside of each potato skin lightly with curry powder. Microwave on 100% (HIGH) 1 minute. Spoon sour cream into skins. Top with chutney and cheese. Makes 2 servings.

# Tri-Color Pepper Appetizers

Pick up and eat like Nachos.

**1 cup green, red and yellow bell pepper strips (¾-inch wide)**
**⅓ cup (1½-oz.) shredded Monterey Jack cheese**
**1 tablespoon coarsely chopped pistachio nuts**
**1 tablespoon canned diced green chilies**
**1 tablespoon sliced green onion**

In a medium-size microwave-safe dish, place bell pepper strips skin side down. Sprinkle with cheese, nuts, green chilies and green onion. Microwave on 100% (HIGH) 1 to 2 minutes or until cheese melts. Makes 2 servings.

# Mexican Chicken Wings

A West Coast version of Buffalo chicken wings.

**8 ounces chicken wings, disjointed**
**½ (1¼-oz.) package taco seasoning**
**mix**

Discard wing tips. In a plastic bag, combine chicken and seasoning mix. Shake to completely coat. Microwave on 100% (HIGH) 1 minute or until cheese begins to melt. Cut in quarters. Serve with salsa and sour cream. Makes 2 servings.

# Chicken Véronique Kabobs

"Véronique" always indicates use of grapes in a recipe.

**1 (4-oz.) boneless skinned chicken**
**breast half, cut in 1-inch cubes**

1 tablespoon Italian salad dressing
12 seedless red or green grapes
6 pineapple chunks
2 tablespoons cream cheese
1 tablespoon thawed frozen orange
  juice concentrate
1 tablespoon dairy sour cream
1 drop hot-pepper sauce

In a small microwave-safe dish, toss chicken with salad dressing. Cover tightly. Microwave on 100% (HIGH) 1½ to 2 minutes or until chicken is done; stir. Refrigerate until cool. On 6 short skewers, alternate chicken, grapes and pineapple chunks. Set aside. To make dip, in a 1-cup glass measure, microwave cream cheese and orange juice on 100% (HIGH) 5 to 10 seconds or until cream cheese is soft. Stir in sour cream and hot sauce. Serve kabobs with dip. Makes 2 servings.

# Mini-Reubens

Leftover corned beef makes great hash.

4 squares crispy rye crackers
Dijon-style mustard

4 small pieces corned beef
2 teaspoons drained sauerkraut
4 (1-inch) squares Swiss cheese

Spread crackers with mustard. Arrange on a microwave-safe serving plate. Place corned beef on crackers, then sauerkraut. Top with cheese. Microwave on 100% (HIGH) 45 seconds or until cheese begins to melt. Makes 2 servings.

# Bacon-Wrapped Watermelon Pickles

No charred wooden picks when appetizers are microwaved!

2 slices bacon, each cut in quarters
4 watermelon pickle squares, each
  cut in half

Place a paper towel on a microwave-safe plate. Wrap a piece of bacon around each pickle square. Secure with wooden picks. Arrange wrapped pickles in a circle on prepared plate. Cover with a paper towel. Microwave on 100% (HIGH) 2 to 3 minutes or until bacon is crisp. Makes 2 servings.

# Oysters Rockefeller

For a quick dip, stir reserved thawed spinach into one-fourth cup sour cream.

**1 (10-oz.) package frozen creamed spinach**
**6 oysters, shells scrubbed**
**Kosher salt**
**Hot-pepper sauce**
**1 tablespoon butter or margarine**
**2 tablespoons grated Parmesan cheese**
**2 tablespoons dry bread crumbs**
**Red caviar, if desired**

On a microwave-safe plate, microwave spinach in package on 50% (MEDIUM) 4 minutes or until thawed. Remove spinach from package. Reserve ½ of spinach for another use. In a microwave-safe dish, arrange oysters in a cartwheel pattern with hinges pointing outward. Cover tightly. Microwave on 100% (HIGH) 1½ minutes or until shells open. Remove shells as they open to avoid overcooking. Cut oyster at muscle to separate from shells; remove from shell. Place an oyster in each top-rounded shell. Pour salt at least ¼-inch thick in center of a microwave-safe plate. Arrange shells in a cartwheel pattern on salt. Pierce each oyster with a fork. Sprinkle each oyster with 1 to 2 drops hot-pepper sauce. Spread spinach over oysters. Set aside. In a small microwave-safe bowl, microwave butter or margarine on 100% (HIGH) 15 seconds or until melted. Remove from oven. Stir in Parmesan cheese and bread crumbs. Sprinkle mixture evenly over spinach on each oyster. Microwave on 70% (MEDIUM-HIGH) 1½ to 2 minutes or until spinach bubbles around edges. Top with red caviar, if desired. Makes 2 servings.

# *Brandy Slush*

Freeze this mix for yourself or to have on hand when guests drop in.

   **2 cups water**
   **¼ cup sugar**
   **2 tablespoons instant tea granules**
   **1 (6-oz.) can frozen lemonade**
      **concentrate, thawed**
   **¼ cup Triple Sec or orange-flavored**
      **liqueur**
   **¼ cup brandy, bourbon or rum**

In a 4-cup glass measure, combine water and sugar. Microwave on 100% (HIGH) 4 to 5 minutes or until mixture comes to a boil. Remove from oven. Stir in tea granules, lemonade concentrate, Triple Sec or orange-flavored liqueur and brandy, bourbon or rum. Pour into a freezer container; cover tightly. Freeze 12 hours. Mixture will be frozen but spoonable due to high alcohol content. Makes 6 servings.

**To Make 1 Serving:**
Scoop ½ cup frozen mixture into a tall 12-ounce glass. Fill glass with cold ginger ale or lemon-lime soda; stir. Garnish with fresh mint and a lemon slice, if desired.

# *Italian Tomato Cup*

Hearty, flavorful and few calories!

**1 (8-oz.) can tomato juice or
    vegetable and tomato juice
Pinch dried leaf oregano
Pinch garlic powder
1 celery stick**

In a 12-ounce microwave-safe mug, mix juice, oregano and garlic. Microwave on

100% (HIGH) 2 minutes; stir. Garnish with celery stick. Makes 1 serving.

# Cinnamon Cocoa

A warm and cozy beverage for a cold night.

**1½ teaspoons unsweetened cocoa powder**
**2 teaspoons sugar**
**⅛ teaspoon ground cinnamon**
**2 tablespoons water**
**1 cup milk**
**⅛ teaspoon vanilla extract**

In a 12-ounce microwave-safe mug, combine cocoa powder, sugar, cinnamon and water. Microwave on 100% (HIGH) 30 seconds. Remove from oven. Stir in milk. Microwave on 100% (HIGH) 2 minutes or until hot. Stir in vanilla. Makes 1 serving.

# Mocha Express

Coffee and cocoa are a pleasing combination.

**1 tablespoon unsweetened cocoa powder**

**2 tablespoons sugar**
**1 teaspoon instant coffee granules**
**3 tablespoons water**
**1 cup milk**
**1 (½″ × 2″) strip orange peel**
**1 tablespoon bourbon**

In a 12-ounce microwave-safe mug, combine cocoa powder, sugar, coffee granules and water. Microwave on 100% (HIGH) 30 seconds. Remove from oven. Stir in milk; add orange peel. Microwave on 100% (HIGH) 2 minutes or until hot. Stir in bourbon. Let stand 1 minute. Remove and discard orange peel. Makes 1 serving.

# *Hot Toddy Mix*

Refrigerate in a covered jar up to two months. Stir into hot cider, coffee or tea.

**¼ cup butter**
**1 cup packed light-brown sugar**
**2 teaspoons granulated sugar**
**½ teaspoon vanilla extract**
**1 teaspoon imitation rum flavoring**
**⅛ teaspoon ground cinnamon**
**Pinch ground nutmeg**

In a custard cup, microwave butter on 70% (MEDIUM-HIGH) 10 seconds to soften. In a blender or a food processor fitted with a metal blade, process butter, light-brown sugar, granulated sugar, vanilla, rum flavoring, cinnamon and nutmeg. Refrigerate in a jar with a tight fitting lid up to 2 months. Makes about 16 servings.

**To Make 1 Serving:**
In a 12-ounce microwave-safe mug, stir 1 tablespoon Hot Toddy Mix into 8 ounces cider, coffee or tea. Microwave on 100% (HIGH) 2 minutes; stir.

# Peach Melba Shake

A liquified version of Peach Melba (ice cream with peaches and raspberry sauce).

> 1 cup water
> 2 tablespoons sugar
> 2 tea bags
> 1 small ripe peach, peeled, sliced or
>   8 slices thawed frozen or canned
>   peaches
> 1½ cups vanilla ice cream
> ½ cup fresh or thawed frozen
>   unsweetned raspberries

In a 2-cup glass measure, microwave water on 100% (HIGH) 3 minutes or until water comes to a boil. Stir in sugar until dissolved. Add tea bags. Let steep 5 minutes. Remove and discard tea bags. Cool to room temperature. In a blender or a food processor fitted with a metal blade, process tea, peaches, ice cream and raspberries until well blended. Serve immediately. Makes 2 servings.

---

*Chef's Tip*
Crisp 2 cups stale potato chips or pretzels by microwaving 15 to 30 seconds. Let stand 2 minutes.

---

# Kahlua Cocoa

---

Kahlua, a coffee-flavored liqueur, is a favorite in coffee. Try it with cocoa!

**1 tablespoon unsweetened cocoa
  powder**
**2 tablespoons sugar**
**2 tablespoons water**
**1 cup milk**
**2 tablespoons Kahlua**
**Whipped cream**

In a 12-ounce microwave-safe mug, combine cocoa powder, sugar and water. Microwave on 100% (HIGH) 30 seconds. Remove from oven. Stir in milk. Microwave on 100% (HIGH) 2 minutes or until hot. Stir in Kahlua. Top with whipped cream. Makes 1 serving.

# Hot Orange Cider

A wonderful hot beverage!

**1 cup apple cider**
**1 tablespoon thawed frozen orange
    juice concentrate**
**2 whole cloves**
**1 (2-inch) piece cinnamon stick**

In a 12-ounce microwave-safe mug, combine cider and orange juice concentrate. Add cloves and cinnamon stick. Microwave on 100% (HIGH) 3 minutes; stir. Remove and discard cloves and cinnamon stick. Makes 1 serving.

# Lemonade Syrup

What's better on a hot day than cold lemonade!

**½ cup water**
**1 cup sugar**
**1 tablespoon grated lemon peel**
**1 cup lemon juice**

In a 4-cup glass measure, combine water and sugar. Microwave on 100% (HIGH) 3 minutes or until sugar dissolves, stirring several times. Remove from oven. Stir in lemon peel. Cool to room temperature. Stir in lemon juice. Refrigerate tightly covered. Makes 4 to 6 servings.

**To Make 1 Serving:**
In a tall glass, mix ⅓ cup Lemonade Syrup and ¾ cup soda water or cold water. Fill glass with ice.

# Sangria

Heating orange and lemon slices releases more juice and fragrant oils.

**1 thin slice orange**
**1 thin slice lemon**

41

**1 teaspoon sugar**
**½ cup chilled dry red wine**
**½ cup chilled club soda**
**Crushed ice**

In a 12-ounce microwave-safe wine glass, microwave orange and lemon slices on 100% (HIGH) 30 seconds to release oils. Remove from oven. Carefully crush fruit with back of a spoon. Sprinkle with sugar. Let stand 5 minutes. Pour in wine and club soda; stir. Add ice. Makes 1 serving.

---

*Chef's Tip*
To mix frozen concentrated juices quickly, remove from can and place in a microwave-safe pitcher. Microwave on 100% (HIGH) 30 to 45 seconds or until soft. Add water and stir.

---

# SOUPS

Soups today are made in just about any flavor or combination of flavors you can imagine. With a microwave oven and a need to create only small amounts, you're in business!

The varieties of fresh vegetable soups are wonderful. Start with appetizing Carrot-Cream Soup, then venture to Hot & Sour Soup. Due to short cooking time for soups in a microwave oven, you'll need to reorganize the traditional cooking order. Cut meat and vegetables in bite-size pieces and microwave separately. Add to the broth and microwave long enough to blend flavors.

There is nothing to match the flavor of homemade chicken soup. Two soups in this chapter are made from my recipe for Basic Chicken Soup. Use Basic Chicken Soup for your own personal recipes as well. This broth, as with most soups, freezes well. Pour a single serving into a plastic freezer container and freeze. When you're hungry for soup, just pop the container in the microwave oven and defrost. Pour into a micro-wave-safe serving bowl, heat and soup is ready!

If you don't have time to make broth from scratch, keep beef and chicken bouillon cubes or granules on your pantry shelf. They are quick flavor enhancers and tasty for a quick soup. Dissolve bouillon in a mug of water, stir in leftover vegetables or meat, and microwave until steaming. Quick soup!

# Swiss Vegetable Bisque

Tasty as well as healthy.

**½ cup coarsely chopped broccoli**
**¼ cup thinly sliced carrot**
**2 tablespoons thinly sliced celery**
**2 tablespoons chopped onion**
**1 tablespoon butter or margarine**
**1 tablespoon all-purpose flour**
**1 cup Basic Chicken Soup, page 34**
**Pinch ground nutmeg**
**¼ cup half and half**
**⅓ cup (1½-oz.) shredded Monterey Jack cheese**

In a small microwave-safe dish, combine broccoli, carrot, celery and onion. Cover tightly. Microwave on 100% (HIGH) 2 to 2½ minutes or until tender. Set aside. In a medium-size microwave-safe bowl, microwave butter or margarine on 100% (HIGH) 15 to 20 seconds or until melted. Remove from oven. Stir in flour until smooth. Microwave on 100% (HIGH) 30 seconds. Remove from oven. Stir in Basic Chicken Soup, nutmeg and half and half. Microwave on 100% (HIGH) 3 minutes or until mixture comes

47

to a boil. Stir in cheese until smooth. Set aside. Drain and discard liquid from vegetables; stir vegetables into bisque. Makes 2 servings.

# Cucumber-Salmon Soup

A delicious soup to enjoy for lunch.

**1 cup peeled diced cucumber**
**2 tablespoons chopped green onion**
**1 tablespoon butter or margarine**
**1½ cups chicken broth**
**1 teaspoon cornstarch**
**¼ teaspoon dried dill weed**
**¼ cup plain yogurt**
**1 (7¾-oz.) can salmon, drained, skin and bones removed and discarded, broken in bite-size pieces**

In a small microwave-safe dish, microwave cucumber, green onion and butter or margarine on 100% (HIGH) 2½ to 3 minutes or until onion is tender. Remove from oven. In a blender or a food processor fitted with a metal blade, process cucumber mixture,

48

chicken broth, cornstarch, dill weed and yo-gurt to a purée. Return to dish. Stir in salmon. Microwave on 100% (HIGH) 2 to 3 minutes or until heated through. Makes 2 servings.

*Chef's Tip*
To add a mild garlic flavor to soup, spear a peeled garlic clove with a wooden pick and drop it into your soup. Remove and discard before serving.

# Chinese Pea Pod Soup

Small tender Chinese pea pods or snow peas can usually be found in the fresh produce or freezer section of your supermarket.

**1 cup chicken broth**
**3 small Chinese pea pods, cut in 1-inch pieces**
**1 teaspoon sliced green onion**
**2 medium-size fresh mushrooms, thinly sliced**
**½ very thin slice gingerroot**

In a microwave-safe serving bowl, combine chicken broth, pea pods, green onion, mushrooms and gingerroot. Microwave on 100% (HIGH) 4 minutes, stirring once. Remove and discard gingerroot. Makes 1 serving.

# *Curried Soup*

A simply elegant soup!

> **1 cup chicken broth**
> **½ cup half and half**
> **¼ to ½ teaspoon curry powder**
> **Dash ground ginger**
> **¼ cup peeled chopped apple**
> **1 tablespoon shredded unsweetened coconut**

In a 4-cup glass measure, combine chicken broth, half and half, curry powder and ginger. Microwave on 100% (HIGH) 3 minutes. Remove from oven. Stir in apple and coconut. Microwave on 100% (HIGH) 1 to 2 minutes or until heated through. Makes 2 servings.

# Carrot-Cream Soup

Broccoli can be substituted for carrots. For a chunky soup, do not purée completely.

**1 cup sliced carrot**
**½ cup sliced celery**
**1 cup chicken broth**
**1 teaspoon chopped fresh parsley**
**½ cup plain yogurt**

Combine carrot and celery in a small microwave-safe dish. Cover tightly. Microwave on 100% (HIGH) 4 to 5 minutes or until tender. In a blender or food processor fitted with a metal blade, process carrot, celery, chicken broth, parsley and yogurt to a purée. Pour into 2 microwave-safe serving bowls. Microwave each on 100% (HIGH) 1 minute; stir. Makes 2 servings.

# Hot & Sour Soup

Tofu is an inexpensive protein alternative to meat.

**2 teaspoons cornstarch**
**1½ cups chicken broth**

4 medium-size fresh mushrooms,
   thinly sliced
2 ounces boneless pork, very thinly
   sliced
1/4 cup bean sprouts
1 1/2 tablespoons white wine vinegar
1 tablespoon soy sauce
1/8 teaspoon red pepper flakes
2 ounces tofu, drained, rinsed, well
   drained, diced
1/4 teaspoon sesame oil
1 tablespoon sliced green onion

In a small microwave-safe casserole dish, dissolve cornstarch in chicken broth. Microwave on 100% (HIGH) 3 minutes or until mixture comes to a boil, stirring several times. Remove from oven. Stir in mushrooms, pork, bean sprouts, vinegar, soy sauce, red pepper flakes and tofu. Cover tightly. Microwave on 100% (HIGH) 3 minutes. Stir in sesame oil. To serve, sprinkle with green onion. Makes 2 servings.

# Jewel Chicken Soup

Colors of the vegetables glisten like jewels in this soup.

**2 (3-oz.) chicken thighs**
**¼ medium-size red bell pepper,**
  **thinly sliced**
**1 small yellow or green zucchini, cut**
  **in Zucchini Blossoms, page 95**
**1 carrot, cut in julienne strips**
**½ cup fresh spinach, torn in small**
  **pieces**
**4 medium-size fresh mushrooms,**
  **thinly sliced**
**2 cups chicken broth**
**1 tablespoon dry white wine**

Place chicken in a small microwave-safe dish. Cover tightly. Microwave on 100% (HIGH) 3½ to 4 minutes or until chicken is no longer pink when cut. Cool to room temperature. Remove skin and debone; cut chicken in ½-inch cubes. Set aside. In a medium-size microwave-safe dish, combine red pepper, zucchini, carrot, spinach and mushrooms. Cover tightly. Microwave on 100% (HIGH) 2 to 2½ minutes or until vegetables are tender-crisp. Remove from oven. Stir in chicken, chicken broth and wine; re-cover. Microwave on 100% (HIGH) 5 minutes; stir. Makes 2 servings.

# *Minestrone*

Top this hearty soup with an ample sprinkling of freshly grated Parmesan cheese.

**¼ cup chopped onion**
**2 tablespoons thinly sliced celery**
**1 small garlic clove, finely chopped**
**1 (8-oz.) can ready-cut peeled**
**   tomatoes**
**¼ cup fine egg noodles**
**¼ cup canned white beans**
**¼ teaspoon dried leaf thyme**
**¼ teaspoon dried leaf oregano**
**4 ounces pepperoni, thinly sliced,**
**   cut in quarters**
**1 cup water**
**1 beef bouillon cube**
**¼ cup (¾-oz.) freshly grated**
**   Parmesan cheese**

In a medium-size microwave-safe dish, combine onion, celery and garlic. Cover tightly. Microwave on 100% (HIGH) 1 to 1½ minutes or until onion is tender. Remove from oven.

Stir in tomatoes with juice, noodles, beans, thyme, oregano, pepperoni and water. Add bouillon cube; re-cover. Microwave on 100% (HIGH) 10 minutes or until noodles are tender, stirring once. Let stand 5 minutes. To serve, sprinkle with cheese. Makes 2 servings.

# Chicken & Dumplings

A childhood favorite, updated for the microwave oven.

**1 cup Basic Chicken Soup, below**
**2 teaspoons dry white wine**
**⅛ teaspoon dried ground rosemary**
**1 teaspoon finely chopped fresh parsley**
**1 small carrot, sliced**
**¼ cup chopped fresh green beans**
**1 tablespoon sliced celery**
**½ cup buttermilk baking mix**
**3 tablespoons milk**

In a small microwave-safe serving bowl, combine Basic Chicken Soup, wine, rosemary, parsley, carrot, green beans and celery. Cover tightly. Microwave on 100% (HIGH) 6 minutes. Set aside. In a small bowl, stir baking mix and milk together to form a sticky dough. Drop dough by table-spoonfuls on top of soup mixture. Microwave on 100% (HIGH) 1 to 2 minutes or until surface of dumplings are dry. Makes 1 serving.

# Basic Chicken Soup

Freeze soup in small amounts for future use.

**1 (6-oz.) chicken breast half**
**3 cups water**
**½ medium-size onion, sliced**
**1 small carrot, coarsely chopped**
**1 garlic clove**
**2 peppercorns**
**1 whole clove**

In a large microwave-safe dish, combine chicken, water, onion, carrot, garlic, peppercorns and clove. Cover tightly. Microwave on 50% (MEDIUM) 30 minutes. Cool to room temperature. Remove and discard garlic, peppercorns and clove. Remove skin and debone chicken breast; shred meat. Stir meat into broth. Makes about 3 cups.

# *Gazpacho*

Traditionally served cold, this soup tastes great served hot, too!

**1 teaspoon olive oil**
**2 tablespoons chopped cucumber**
**2 tablespoons chopped green bell pepper**
**¼ cup chopped tomato**
**¾ cup tomato juice**
**1 teaspoon wine vinegar**

In a microwave-safe serving bowl, combine olive oil, cucumber, bell pepper and tomato. Cover tightly. Microwave on 100% (HIGH) 2 minutes. Remove from oven. Stir in tomato juice and vinegar. To serve hot, re-cover; microwave on 100% (HIGH) 2 minutes more. To serve cold, refrigerate 1 hour or stir in 3 ice cubes until soup is just chilled; discard remaining ice cubes. Makes 1 serving.

# French Onion Soup

Enjoy good French onion soup at home!

**1 tablespoon butter or margarine**
**1 medium-size onion, thinly sliced**
**¼ teaspoon sugar**
**1 cup water**
**1½ beef boullion cubes, crumbled**
**⅛ teaspoon Worcestershire sauce**
**1 teaspoon brandy**
**1 bay leaf**
**1 slice French bread, toasted**
**¼ cup (1-oz.) shredded Swiss cheese**
**1 teaspoon freshly grated Parmesan
   cheese**

In a microwave-safe serving bowl, micro-wave butter or margarine, onion and sugar on 100% (HIGH) 4 minutes or until onion is thoroughly cooked, stirring several times. Set aside. In a 1-cup glass measure, micro-wave water and boullion cubes on 100% (HIGH) 2 minutes. Stir until boullion cubes dissolve. Mix broth, Worcestershire sauce and brandy into onion mixture. Add bay leaf. Microwave on 100% (HIGH) 4 minutes. Remove from oven. Remove and discard bay leaf. Float bread on soup. Sprinkle with Swiss cheese, then Parmesan cheese. Microwave on 100% (HIGH) 1 to 1½ minutes or until cheeses melt. Makes 1 serving.

# *SALADS*

Initially you might wonder why a chapter on salads is included in a microwave cookbook. But consider how many ingredients are often cooked before being combined in a salad and you won't be surprised. Microwave ovens are a great help to chicken salads when you can microwave a chicken breast and have it salad-ready in 5 minutes. Spinach Salad with Hot Soy Dressing is an obvious choice and never so quick or easy as when the dressing is microwaved.

Salads can be served at all temperatures, from hot to room temperature to chilled. Warm Salmon Salad is one of my favorite contemporary salads. Old-time favorite gelatin salads are good choices for a microwave oven. Water or liquid to dissolve the gelatin is microwaved on 100% (HIGH) until it boils. If using sugar-sweetened gelatins, use a measuring cup or bowl at least twice the capacity of the liquid. Sugar heats up very quickly and causes the mixture to boil rapidly and voluminously.

Microwaving pasta and quick-cooking rice takes about the same length of time as it would conventionally. In a large bowl, bring water to a boil. Add beef or chicken bouillon to the cooking water for more flavor. Stir in pasta or rice and microwave until tender, stirring occasionally; drain. Toss in other ingredients and you've saved washing a pan.

Salads are versatile enough to be served at the beginning of a meal as an appetizer or with the meal—family style. Europeans serve a light salad after the entrée, just before dessert. Some salads are so substantial they are a meal in themselves. Whichever you choose, appetizer or entrée, you'll find many interesting salads in this chapter.

# Strawberry-Banana Cantaloupe

A very impressive salad.

**1 (3-oz.) package strawberry-flavored gelatin**
**2 cups water**
**½ cantaloupe, peeled, seeded**
**½ banana**
**Lettuce leaves**

In a 4-cup glass measure, combine gelatin and 1 cup of water. Microwave on 100% (HIGH) 3 minutes or until mixture comes to a boil. Stir until gelatin is completely dissolved. Stir in remaining 1 cup of water. Set aside. Cut a thin slice off bottom of cantaloupe so cantaloupe sets level; place on a plate. Peel and slice banana. Arrange in cantaloupe cavity. Pour gelatin to top of cantaloupe. Chill remaining gelatin for other use. Refrigerate cantaloupe until gelatin is completely set. Cut cantaloupe in half lengthwise. Serve on lettuce leaves. Makes 2 servings.

# Cinnamon Spice Ambrosia

Serve as a nice light dessert, too.

**½ cup sugar**
**¼ cup water**
**½ cup Chablis wine**
**1 whole clove**
**1 (2-inch) piece cinnamon stick**
**2 oranges, peeled, white membrane removed, sliced crosswise**
**½ cup shredded unsweetened coconut**
**1 banana**
**Lettuce leaves**

In a 2-cup glass measure, combine sugar, water, wine, clove and cinnamon stick. Microwave on 100% (HIGH) 2½ minutes. Remove from oven. Remove and discard clove and cinnamon stick. Stir until sugar dissolves. Set syrup aside. In a medium-size bowl, combine oranges and coconut. Pour syrup over oranges and coconut. Cover tightly. Refrigerate at least 1 hour or overnight. Slice banana; fold into orange mixture. Serve on lettuce leaves. Makes 2 servings.

# Asparagus & Endive Salad with Curry Dressing

A light refreshing salad, serve with Crispy Cod Fillets, page 80.

**8 asparagus spears, trimmed**
**¼ cup dairy sour cream**
**1 tablespoon mayonnaise**
**¼ teaspoon curry powder**
**1 teaspoon finely chopped green onion**
**1 small head Belgian endive, separated in leaves**
**1 tablespoon shredded Cheddar cheese**

Place asparagus spears on a microwave-safe plate. Cover tightly. Microwave on 100% (HIGH) 1 to 1½ minutes or until tender-crisp. Cool under cold running water. Drain on a paper towel. Set aside. To make dressing, in a small bowl, combined sour cream, mayonnaise, curry powder and green onion. Set aside. Place endive on 2 salad plates. Top with asparagus. Spoon dressing over aspar-

67

agus. Sprinkle with cheese. Makes 2 servings.

# Salad Croutons

A tasty topping for soup, too! Store leftover croutons in a plastic bag.

**2 teaspoons butter or margarine**
**1 slice bread, cut in ½-inch cubes**
**1 or all of the following: ¼ teaspoon**
  **Italian herb seasoning**
**2 teaspoons grated Parmesan cheese**
**Dash garlic powder**

In a small microwave-safe bowl, microwave butter or margarine on 100% (HIGH) 15 seconds or until melted. Stir in bread cubes, then sprinkle with herb seasoning, cheese and/or garlic powder. Microwave on 100% (HIGH) 1½ to 2 minutes or until dry; stir. Makes about ¾ cup.

*Chef's Tip*
To dry bread crumbs, spread ½ cup bread crumbs (1 slice bread) in a glass pie plate. Microwave on 100% (HIGH) 1 minute or until dry, stirring once.

# Salad Niçoise

Niçoise means "in the style of Nice," a beautiful city on the French Riviera.

1 (5-oz.) baking potato, pierced
6 fresh green beans
2 cups romaine lettuce, torn in small
 pieces
6 cucumber slices
½ tomato, cut in wedges
6 pitted black olives
1 (3¼-oz.) can tuna, drained
4 anchovy fillets
1 hard-cooked egg, finely chopped
Vinegar
Olive oil

Place potato in microwave oven. Microwave on 100% (HIGH) 3 minutes. Turn potato over. Microwave on 100% (HIGH) 1 to 3 minutes more or until potato gives slightly when squeezed. Wrap in foil. Let stand 5 minutes. Wrap green beans in plastic wrap. Microwave on 100% (HIGH) 1 minute. Set aside. Place lettuce on 2 salad plates. Arrange green beans, cucumber, tomato and olives around edge of lettuce. Peel and dice potato. Place in center of vegetables. Arrange tuna around potatoes. Sprinkle with egg. Crisscross 2 anchovies on top of potatoes. Serve with vinegar and olive oil. Makes 2 servings.

# Pepper Strip Salad

Refrigerate up to 4 days.

**1 red bell pepper, pierced**
**1 yellow bell pepper, pierced**
**1 green bell pepper, pierced**
**¼ cup olive oil**
**3 tablespoons rice vinegar**
**2 tablespoons fresh basil leaves, finely chopped or 1 teaspoon dried leaf basil, if desired**
**Lettuce leaves**

Wrap each pepper individually in plastic wrap. Place in microwave oven. Microwave on 100% (HIGH) 3 minutes. Do not unwrap. Cool to room temperature. Peel skin from peppers. If skin does not peel easily, rewrap and microwave on 100% (HIGH) 30 seconds more. Remove and discard stem and seeds. Slice peppers lengthwise in ½-inch-wide strips. In a medium-size bowl, combine peppers, olive oil, vinegar and basil, if desired. Cover tightly. Refrigerate at least 1 hour or overnight. Place lettuce on 2 serving plates. Arrange pepper strips over lettuce. Makes 2 servings.

# Spinach Salad with Hot Soy Dressing

Rinse spinach leaves in cold water to remove sand and dirt.

> 2 slices bacon, cut in small pieces
> ½ small onion, finely chopped
> 8 fresh mushrooms, thinly sliced
> ¼ cup rice vinegar or white wine vinegar
> 1 tablespoon soy sauce
> 2 teaspoons sugar
> ⅛ teaspoon pepper
> 1 bunch spinach, rinsed, torn in bite-size pieces
> 1 small tomato, cut in wedges
> ½ cup bean sprouts

To make dressing, place bacon in a medium-size microwave-safe dish. Cover with a paper towel. Microwave on 100% (HIGH) 2 minutes or until crisp. Remove from oven. Stir in onion and mushrooms. Microwave on 100% (HIGH) 1½ to 2 minutes or until onion and mushrooms are tender-crisp. Whisk in vinegar, soy sauce, sugar and pepper. Add spinach, tomato and bean sprouts. Toss with dressing. Serve immediately. Makes 2 servings.

# Cilantro Corn Salad

An unlikely combination of ingredients with a wonderful flavor.

½ (10-oz.) package frozen cut corn
¼ cup chopped red bell pepper
2 tablespoons chopped green onion
¼ cup finely chopped fresh cilantro
  (Chinese parsley or coriander)
3 tablespoons vegetable oil
2 tablespoons rice vinegar
1 teaspoon Dijon-style mustard

Place corn in a small microwave-safe dish. Cover tightly. Microwave on 100% (HIGH) 2 to 2½ minutes or until thawed. Stir in bell pepper, green onion and cilantro. Set aside. To make dressing, in a small bowl, whisk oil, vinegar and mustard. Toss vegetables with dressing. Cover tightly. Refrigerate 30 minutes before serving. Makes 2 servings.

# German Potato Salad

Serve warm. If prepared ahead, reheat just before serving.

**2 (5-oz.) baking potatoes, pierced**
**2 slices bacon, chopped**
**½ medium-size onion, chopped**
**1 teaspoon all-purpose flour**
**1 tablespoon sugar**
**3 tablespoons rice vinegar**
**2 tablespoons water**
**Salt**
**Pepper**

Place potatoes in microwave oven. Microwave on 100% (HIGH) 3 minutes. Turn potatoes over. Microwave on 100% (HIGH) 3 to 5 minutes more or until potatoes give slightly when squeezed. Wrap in foil. Let stand 5 minutes. To make dressing, in a medium-size microwave-safe dish, combine bacon and onion. Cover with a paper towel. Microwave on 100% (HIGH) 2 to 2½ minutes or until bacon is crisp. Stir to break up bacon. Whisk in flour, sugar, vinegar and water. Peel and dice potatoes. Add potatoes. Toss with dressing. Season to taste with salt and pepper. Makes 2 servings.

---

*Chef's Tip*
For best results when microwaving, choose a potato with recommended recipe weight. Potatoes of the same size can vary in weight depending on variety and water content.

---

# Warm Mussel & Pasta Salad

---

Either New Zealand mussels or black mussels work well in this salad.

**12 mussels, shells scrubbed, beards removed**
**½ cup dry white wine**
**¼ teaspoon dried leaf tarragon**
**¼ cup olive oil**
**2 tablespoons white wine vinegar**
**1 tablespoon chopped fresh parsley**
**1 teaspoon Dijon-style mustard**

½ small cucumber, cut in half
  lengthwise, seeded, thinly sliced
1½ cups cooked spinach fettuccine,
  drained
1 small bunch radicchio or 1 small
  head curly leaf lettuce
1 ounce red caviar

Place mussels in a large microwave-safe dish. Add wine and tarragon. Cover tightly. Microwave on 100% (HIGH) 4 to 5 minutes or just until mussels open. Remove mussels as they open to avoid overcooking. Discard any unopened mussels. Set aside. To make dressing, in a large bowl, combine olive oil, vinegar, parsley and mustard. Add cucumber and fettuccine. Toss to completely coat pasta with dressing. Arrange radicchio or lettuce on 2 serving plates. Spoon pasta mixture over lettuce. Arrange mussels in shells around pasta on each plate. Sprinkle pasta with caviar. Makes 2 servings.

# Curry Seafood Salad

Sole, turbot or cod are good types of fish for this salad.

**8 ounces fish fillets**
**3 tablespoons olive oil**
**1 tablespoon white wine vinegar**
**⅛ to ¼ teaspoon curry powder**
**¼ teaspoon salt**
**½ cup thinly sliced celery**
**½ cup unpeeled chopped apple**
**2 tablespoons raisins**
**Lettuce leaves**
**1 tablespoon finely sliced green onion**

Wrap fillets in plastic wrap. Place in microwave oven. Microwave on 100% (HIGH) 1½ to 2½ minutes or until fish begins to flake. Let stand, wrapped, 5 minutes. To make dressing, in a medium-size bowl, whisk olive oil, vinegar, curry powder and salt. Set aside. Using a fork, flake fillets. Add fish, celery, apple and raisins to dressing; toss. Cover tightly. Refrigerate salad 30 minutes. Arrange lettuce on 2 plates. Spoon salad over lettuce. Sprinkle with green onion. Makes 2 servings.

# Warm Salmon Salad

If fresh shiitake mushrooms are not available, use four ounces button mushrooms.

**3 ounces fresh salmon, bone and skin removed and discarded, cut in 2-inch chunks**
**4 fresh shiitake mushrooms, sliced**
**1 green onion, finely sliced**
**2 tablespoons olive oil**
**3 tablespoons rice vinegar or white wine vinegar**
**1 tablespoon Dijon-style mustard**
**1 tablespoon finely chopped fresh cilantro (Chinese parsley or coriander)**
**1½ cups bite-size pieces romaine or other dark green lettuce**

In a medium-size microwave-safe dish, combine salmon, mushrooms and onion. Cover tightly. Microwave on 100% (HIGH) 1½ to 2 minutes or until onion is tender. Let stand, covered, 3 minutes. Set aside. To make dressing, in a medium-size bowl, whisk olive oil, vinegar and mustard until well blended. Add cilantro and lettuce. Toss with dressing. Arrange lettuce mixture on a serving plate. Top with salmon mixture. Makes 1 serving.

# Tuna Curry Aspic

Top each serving with a dollop of mayonnaise.

**1 (¼-oz.) envelope unflavored gelatin**
**1 cup chicken broth**
**¼ cup mayonnaise**
**1 teaspoon curry powder**
**1 teaspoon lemon juice**
**1 cup cooked rice**
**1 (3¼-oz.) can tuna, drained, flaked**
**2 tablespoons chopped peanuts**
**1 tablespoon chopped green onion**
**1 tablespoon chopped celery**

In a small microwave-safe bowl, sprinkle gelatin over chicken broth. Let stand 5 minutes. Microwave on 100% (HIGH) 2½ minutes. Stir until gelatin dissolves. Cool to room temperature. In a medium-size bowl, combine mayonnaise, curry powder, lemon juice, rice, tuna, peanuts, green onion and celery. Stir in gelatin. Pour into a 3-cup mold. Refrigerate 12 hours or until completely firm. Unmold to serve. Makes 2 servings.

# Confetti Rice Salad

Serve with chicken or fish.

**½ cup water**
**½ cup quick-cooking rice**
**1 recipe Oregano Dressing, page 47**
**2 tablespoons shredded carrot**
**1 tablespoon finely chopped red or green bell pepper**
**1 tablespoon finely chopped green onion**
**1 teaspoon sunflower seeds**

In a 4-cup glass measure, microwave water on 100% (HIGH) 1½ to 2 minutes or until boiling. Remove from oven. Stir in rice. Cover tightly. Cool to room temperature. Prepare Oregano Dressing as directed. Stir in Oregano Dressing, carrot, bell pepper and green onion. Re-cover; refrigerate 30 minutes. To serve, sprinkle with sunflower seeds. Makes 2 servings.

# Primavera Salad

Brief microwaving steams vegetables to a tender-crisp texture and brings out vibrant color.

> 1 cup broccoli flowerets
> 1 small carrot, thinly sliced
> 8 Chinese pea pods
> ¼ cup thinly sliced red bell pepper
> 1 cup cooked macaroni shells,
>    drained, cooled
> ½ cup dairy sour cream
> 1 teaspoon lemon juice
> 1 small garlic clove, crushed
> 1 teaspoon chopped fresh dill

In a medium-size microwave-safe dish, combine broccoli, carrot, pea pods and bell pepper. Cover tightly. Microwave on 100% (HIGH) 1½ to 2 minutes or until tender-crisp. Rinse vegetables under cold running water; drain. In a small bowl, combine vegetables and pasta. Set aside. To make dressing, in a small bowl, combine sour cream, lemon juice, garlic and dill. Toss vegetables and pasta with dressing. Makes 2 servings.

# Dressings & Vinegars

## Citrus Dressing

**1 teaspoon cornstarch**
**½ cup unsweetened pineapple juice**
**¼ cup orange juice**
**1 teaspoon lemon juice**
**1 tablespoon honey**
**1 teaspoon poppy seeds**

In a 1-cup glass measure, dissolve cornstarch in pineapple juice. Stir in orange juice, lemon juice and honey. Microwave on 100% (HIGH) 3 minutes or until slightly thickened, stirring after 2 minutes. Stir in poppy seeds. Chill before serving. Makes ¾ cup.

## Fruit Salad Dressing

**1 tablespoon sugar**
**1 teaspoon cornstarch**
**1 egg yolk**
**½ cup unsweetened pineapple juice**
**¼ teaspoon vanilla extract**

In a 2-cup glass measure, combine sugar and cornstarch. Whisk in egg yolk, then pine-

81

apple juice. Microwave on 100% (HIGH) 3 minutes or until slightly thickened, stirring after 2 minutes. Cool to room temperature. Stir in vanilla. Makes ⅔ cup.

## Basil Dressing

¼ **cup sugar**
**2 tablespoons all-purpose flour**
⅔ **cup water**
**1 egg yolk**
⅓ **cup white wine vinegar**
½ **teaspoon dry mustard**
½ **teaspoon dried leaf basil**

In a 2-cup glass measure, mix sugar and flour. Whisk in water, then egg yolk, vinegar, mustard and basil. Microwave on 100% (HIGH) 3 minutes, stirring after 2 minutes. Cover tightly. Refrigerate up to 1 week. Makes 1¼ cups.

## Fresh Herb Vinegar

½ **cup loosely packed fresh basil,**
  **rosemary or tarragon leaves**
**1 garlic clove, if desired**
**1 cup white wine vinegar**

Rinse herbs thoroughly; pat dry. Pack herbs, and garlic if desired, in a glass jar. In a 2-cup glass measure, microwave vinegar on 100% (HIGH) 3 minutes or until vinegar comes to a boil. Pour over herbs. Cover tightly. Let stand overnight at room temperature. Strain into a sterilized glass bottle. Cap tightly. Makes 1 cup.

*Raspberry Vinegar*

**2 pints raspberries**
**1 cup white wine vinegar**

Crush berries in a ceramic bowl. Set aside. In a 2-cup glass measure, microwave vinegar on 100% (HIGH) 3 minutes or until vinegar comes to a boil. Pour over berries. Cover tightly. Let stand overnight at room temperature. Strain into a sterilized glass bottle. Cap tightly. Makes 1¼ cups.

# Spinach & Pasta Salad

Fresh spinach adds color and flavor. Serve with warm garlic bread.

> 2 cups water
> 1¼ teaspoons salt, if desired
> ⅓ cup (2-oz.) spiral macaroni
> ½ cup fresh spinach, torn in bite-size pieces
> 6 Chinese pea pods, cut crosswise in thirds
> ¼ cup diced tomato
> 1 tablespoon chopped pistachio nuts
> 1 tablespoon grated Parmesan cheese

*Oregano Dressing:*
> 1½ tablespoons olive oil
> 1½ tablespoons white wine vinegar
> ¼ teaspoon dried leaf oregano

Prepare Oregano Dressing. Set aside. In a 4-cup glass measure, microwave water, and salt if desired, on 100% (HIGH) 5 to 6 minutes or until water comes to a boil. Remove from oven. Stir in macaroni. Microwave on

100% (HIGH) 2 minutes. Stir; test for doneness. If needed, microwave on 100% (HIGH) in 1 minute increments until pasta is tender; drain. In a medium-size bowl, toss pasta and spinach with dressing. Cool to room temperature. Wrap pea pods in plastic wrap. Microwave on 100% (HIGH) 30 seconds. Toss pea pods and tomato with spinach and pasta. Sprinkle with nuts and cheese. Makes 2 servings.

**Oregano Dressing:**
In a small bowl, whisk olive oil, vinegar and oregano until well blended.

# MEATS

Using a microwave oven to prepare small amounts of meat gives you the versatility to prepare only one serving of Veal al Fresco or to make two servings of Beef Stroganoff; eat one now and effortlessly reheat the second later. You'll find it easy to keep interest high as you explore many meat cuts which can be successfully microwaved. In this chapter, you'll find everything from "Stir-fry" to pot roast. "Stir-fry" is not really fried. Thinly cut meat and vegetables are quickly microwaved to give a tender, colorful dish. The trick to microwaving a pot roast is to use a tightly covered microwave-safe casserole dish or a pierced plastic cooking bag. Microwave on 30% (MEDIUM-LOW) to 50% (MEDIUM) to give meat time to tenderize.

Microwaving meat is one area from which people sometimes shy away. Several tips are included in this chapter to give you tasty, tender and attractive results. After a few successes, your confidence will be bolstered and you will be preparing a wide variety of favorite meat entrées quickly and conveniently.

Ground meat, always an economical and versatile favorite, is especially suited to microwave cookery. Serve Enchiladas or satisfy a hearty appetite in minutes by preparing Make-Ahead Lasagna. Ground meat can be microwaved in a number of ways. For quick cooking and grease removal, break up ground beef in a microwave-safe plastic colander set over a microwave-safe bowl. Microwave on 100% (HIGH), stirring once or twice to break ground beef in small pieces. Grease will drain in the bowl below. When preparing a meatloaf, use a glass or plastic ring mold. Or form the meat in a donut shape and microwave in a pie plate. Patties and meatballs can be microwaved on a microwave-safe roasting rack set in a microwave-safe dish to catch drippings or in a microwave-safe casserole dish.

When microwaving chops or steaks, use a shallow casserole dish to hold juices. Arrange these cuts of meat with the thickest part toward the outside, bones toward the center.

A wide shallow container makes turning or rearranging easier.

Knowing which covering to use on meats when microwaving is an important part of getting perfect results. A loose cover of wax paper is recommended for reheating, preventing spattering and holding some heat in without steaming when roasting. Less tender cuts of meat need plastic wrap, a cooking bag or a tight fitting lid to hold in steam and tenderize the meat. Always be careful when removing tight fitting covers. Remove away from you to allow steam to escape.

Cover any part of the meat that cooks faster than the rest with a small piece of foil. Press the foil close to the meat to prevent small pieces from sticking out. This shields the cooked part from receiving more microwaves so the rest of the meat can continue to cook. An important safeguard is to always have more food exposed than foil.

# *Enchiladas*

Prepare small amounts of enchilada sauce by combining a few tablespoons from a dry packaged mix with water.

**8 ounces ground beef, crumbled**
**2 (6-inch) corn tortillas**
**½ cup prepared enchilada sauce**
**1 cup shredded lettuce**
**¼ cup chopped green onion**
**2 teaspoons finely chopped fresh cilantro, (Chinese parsley or coriander), if desired**
**½ cup (2-oz.) shredded Cheddar cheese**

In a microwave-safe plastic colander set over a microwave-safe bowl, microwave beef on 100% power (HIGH) 2 to 3 minutes or until beef is no longer pink. Stir to break up beef. Set aside. Pour sauce into a pie plate. Dip tortillas into sauce to coat both sides. Place flat in a microwave-safe serving dish. Sprinkle beef, lettuce, green onion and cilantro down center of tortillas. Bring both sides over tops. Turn over, seam side down. Top with remaining sauce. Sprinkle with cheese.

Microwave on 100% (HIGH) 1½ to 2 minutes or until cheese melts. Makes 1 serving.

# Make-Ahead Lasagna

Preparing ahead gives flavors time to blend and saves last minute preparation.

1 (7¾-oz.) can tomato sauce
½ teaspoon dried leaf oregano
¼ teaspoon dried leaf thyme
1 small garlic clove, minced
6 cooked lasagna noodles, drained
8 ounces ground beef, crumbled
½ cup small curd cottage cheese
¼ cup dairy sour cream
4 ounces Monterey Jack cheese, sliced
¼ cup (¾-oz.) grated Parmesan cheese

In a small bowl, combine tomato sauce, oregano, thyme and garlic. Set aside. Layer 3 noodles in an 8½" × 4½" × 2½" (5 cup) microwave-safe glass loaf pan. Top with ½ of beef. Layer with ½ of cottage cheese, sour cream, Monterey Jack cheese and sauce. Repeat procedure with remaining beef, cottage cheese, sour cream, Monterey Jack cheese and sauce. Cover tightly. Microwave on 50% (**MEDIUM**) 9 to 10 minutes. Sprinkle with Parmesan cheese. Let stand 5 minutes. Makes 2 servings.

*Chef's Tip*
Grill extra hamburgers, ribs or chicken while coals are hot. Undercook slightly and freeze. Defrost and finish by microwaving.

# *Fajitas*

Easy to prepare and a welcome flavor change.

**12 ounces beef sirloin steak or boneless skinned chicken breast, thinly sliced across grain**
**3 drops hot-pepper sauce**
**⅛ teaspoon chili powder**
**½ cup salsa**
**¼ cup sliced onion**
**½ cup chopped tomato**
**2 (10-inch) flour tortillas**
**¼ cup dairy sour cream**
**¼ cup guacamole**

Place beef or chicken in a small microwave-safe casserole dish. Cover tightly. Microwave on 100% (HIGH) 3 minutes. Remove from oven. Stir to separate. Stir in hot-pepper sauce, chili powder, salsa, onion and tomato; re-cover. Microwave on 100% (HIGH) 2 minutes. Line bottom of microwave oven with paper towels. Lay tortillas overlapping on paper towels. Microwave on 100% (HIGH) 10 seconds. Spoon beef or chicken mixture down center of tortillas. Top with guacamole and sour cream. Fold tortilla over filling. Makes 2 servings.

# Spicy Beef in Pita Bread

Pita bread is a flat round bread available in most supermarkets.

> 1 medium-size onion, finely chopped
> 1 large garlic clove, minced
> ½ teaspoon paprika
> ¼ teaspoon hot-pepper sauce
> ¼ teaspoon salt
> 8 ounces lean beef top round, trimmed, diced
> 1 small tomato, finely chopped
> 2 tablespoons minced fresh parsley

**2 pita bread rounds**
**½ cup plain yogurt**

In a small microwave-safe glass bowl, combine onion, garlic, paprika, hot-pepper sauce and salt. Cover loosely. Microwave on 100% (HIGH) 2 to 2½ minutes or until onion is tender, stirring once. Remove from oven. Mix in beef, tomato and parsley. Microwave on 100% (HIGH) 2½ to 3 minutes or until beef is no longer pink, stirring once. Remove from oven. Place a paper towel in microwave oven. Place bread on paper towel. Microwave on 100% (HIGH) 20 seconds. Cut in half crosswise. Pull bread apart to form a pocket. Spoon beef mixture into pockets. Top with yogurt. Serve immediately. Makes 2 servings.

# Sukiyaki

Any assortment of vegetables can be used in this dish.

**8 ounces beef sirloin steak, cut**
  **across grain in thin diagonal (2″ ×**
  **½″) slices**
**¼ cup soy sauce**

**2 tablespoons ketchup**
**1 teaspoon sugar**
**1 small onion, thinly sliced**
**¼ green bell pepper, thinly sliced**
**¼ cup thinly diagonally sliced celery**
**4 medium-size fresh mushrooms,**
  **thinly sliced**
**2 green onions, cut in 1-inch pieces**
**1 cup hot cooked rice**

In a 2-quart microwave-safe casserole dish, combine beef, soy sauce, ketchup and sugar. Cover tightly. Microwave on 100% (HIGH) 2 minutes. Remove from oven. Stir in onion, bell pepper, celery, mushrooms and green onions; re-cover. Microwave on 100% (HIGH) 2 to 3 minutes or until vegetables are tender-crisp. Serve over rice. Makes 2 servings.

---

*Chef's Tip*
Mix recipe ingredients in an oven cooking bag; place in a glass-ceramic utensil to microwave. This makes preparation for microwave cooking easy and convenient and eliminates the need for additional dishes.

---

# Mediterranean Artichokes

A grapefruit spoon works well to scrape the fuzzy choke from an artichoke heart.

2 (10-oz.) artichokes
2 tablespoons butter or margarine
1 tablespoon all-purpose flour
½ medium-size onion, finely chopped
8 ounces beef top sirloin steak, trimmed, diced
¼ teaspoon salt
¼ teaspoon ground cinnamon
⅛ teaspoon pepper
2 tablespoons pine nuts
1 teaspoon minced fresh parsley
2 tablespoons diced tomato
¼ cup dairy sour cream or plain yogurt

Slice off top 1-inch of artichoke so top is flat. Using scissors, snip off point from each leaf. Rinse under cool water. Drain, but do not shake off water. Wrap individually in plastic wrap. Place artichokes in microwave oven upside down. Microwave on 100% (HIGH) 7 to 8 minutes or until heart is nearly tender when pierced from bottom. Do not unwrap. Set aside. In a 2-quart microwave-safe dish, microwave butter or margarine on 100% (HIGH) 20 to 25 seconds or until melted. Remove from oven. Stir in flour until dissolved. Add onion. Cover tightly. Microwave on 100% (HIGH) 2 minutes, stirring once. Remove from oven. Stir in beef, salt, cinnamon, pepper, nuts and parsley. Microwave on 100% (HIGH) 2 to 3 minutes or until beef is no longer pink; stirring once. Set aside. Unwrap artichokes. Spread artichoke leaves slightly. Remove soft center leaves. Using a spoon, carefully scrape fuzzy choke from heart. Spoon beef mixture into artichokes. Place in a 2-quart microwave-safe dish. Cover tightly. Microwave on 100% (HIGH) 3 to 4 minutes or until heated through. Garnish with a ring of tomato. Serve with sour cream or yogurt. Makes 2 servings.

# Veal al Fresco

Light, fresh-tasting and really fast to prepare.

**2 teaspoons butter or margarine**
**¼ teaspoon Worcestershire sauce**
**1 (4-oz.) veal cutlet, pounded ⅛-inch**
  **thick**
**2 slices tomato**
**2 slices avocado**
**¼ cup (1-oz.) shredded Swiss cheese**
**3 to 4 large spinach leaves**

In a glass pie plate, microwave butter or margarine on 100% (HIGH) 15 seconds. Remove from oven. Stir in Worcestershire sauce. Coat both sides of veal in butter mixture. Microwave on 100% (HIGH) 1 to 1½ minutes or until tender. Remove from oven. Top veal with tomato and avocado. Sprinkle with cheese. Microwave on 100% (HIGH) 30 to 45 seconds or until cheese melts. Serve on spinach leaves. Makes 1 serving.

# Savory Liver & Mushrooms

A quick dish for liver lovers.

1 tablespoon butter or margarine
8 ounces beef liver, cut in narrow
   strips
½ medium-size onion, chopped
½ stalk celery, chopped
3 medium-size fresh mushrooms,
   thinly sliced
¼ teaspoon salt
⅛ teaspoon pepper
¼ teaspoon dried leaf oregano
⅛ teaspoon dried leaf thyme
⅛ teaspoon crushed dried leaf
   rosemary
1 tablespoon all-purpose flour
¼ cup dry white wine
¼ cup dairy sour cream
1 cup hot cooked rice or noodles

In a small microwave-safe casserole dish, microwave butter or margarine on 100% (HIGH) 15 seconds. Remove from oven. Stir in liver, onion, celery and mushrooms. Cover tightly. Microwave on 100% (HIGH)

3 minutes. Remove from oven. Stir in salt, pepper, oregano, thyme and rosemary. Set aside. In a 1-cup measure, stir flour into wine. Stir into liver mixture. Microwave on 100% (HIGH) 1½ minutes. Blend in sour cream. Serve over hot rice or noodles. Makes 2 servings.

# Beef Cordon Bleu

An elegant entrée for two.

**2 thin slices prosciutto or ham**
**2 (3″ × ½″ × ½″) sticks Monterey**
    **Jack cheese**
**2 (4-oz.) beef sirloin steaks, pounded**
    **⅛-inch thick**
**1 egg**
**1 tablespoon water**
**¼ cup fine dry bread crumbs**
**1 tablespoon butter**
**1 tablespoon dry white wine**
**Minced fresh parsley**

Roll prosciutto or ham around each cheese stick. Place in center of beef. Fold beef over envelope-style. Secure with a wooden pick. In a small bowl, beat egg and water. Dip beef rolls in egg mixture. Coat with bread crumbs. In a glass pie plate, microwave butter on 100% (HIGH) 15 to 20 seconds or until melted. Roll beef in butter. Microwave on 100% (HIGH) 3 to 3½ minutes or until beef is no longer pink. Remove to a serving platter. Add wine to drippings in pie plate. Swirl; drizzle over beef. Sprinkle with parsley. Makes 2 servings.

# Sweetbreads à la Suisse

If you haven't tried sweetbreads before, you're in for a real treat!

**1 pound beef sweetbreads, pierced**
**¾ cup water**
**1 tablespoon lemon juice**
**2 tablespoons butter or margarine**
**2 tablespoons all-purpose flour**
**¾ cup milk**
**⅓ cup dry vermouth**
**⅛ teaspoon salt**
**2 dashes white pepper**
**1 chicken bouillon cube, crumbled**
**Minced fresh parsley**

Place sweetbreads in a 2-quart microwave-safe dish. Pour water and lemon juice over sweetbreads. Cover tightly. Microwave on 100% (HIGH) 10 minutes or until no pink remains, turning sweetbreads over and rearranging halfway through cooking. Drain; cool to room temperature. Remove membrane, tubes and gristle. Separate or cut sweetbreads in bite-size pieces. Set aside. In a 4-cup glass measure, microwave butter or margarine and flour on 100% (HIGH) 1 minute. Remove from oven. Blend well. Stir in milk, vermouth, salt and pepper. Add bouillon cube. Microwave on 100% (HIGH) 3 to 4 minutes or until sauce is thick and smooth, stirring twice. Remove from oven. Stir in sweetbreads. Microwave on 100% (HIGH) 1 minute or until heated through. Sprinkle with parsley. Makes 2 servings.

# Beef Stroganoff

My favorite for the microwave oven.

**8 ounces beef sirloin steak, trimmed, thinly sliced across grain**
**4 ounces fresh mushrooms, sliced**
**½ small onion, sliced**

2 teaspoons all-purpose flour
1 teaspoon ketchup
¼ teaspoon dry mustard
⅛ teaspoon salt
2 tablespoons water
2 tablespoons dry red wine
1 beef bouillon cube, crumbled
⅓ cup dairy sour cream
1 cup hot cooked rice or noodles

In a 1-quart microwave-safe casserole dish, sprinkle beef, mushrooms and onion with flour. Stir in ketchup, mustard, salt, water and wine. Add bouillon cube. Cover tightly. Microwave on 100% (HIGH) 2 minutes. Stir until bouillon cube dissolves; re-cover. Microwave on 100% (HIGH) 3 minutes more or until beef is no longer pink. Do not overcook or meat will become tough. Stir in sour cream. Serve over rice or noodles. Makes 2 servings.

# Teriyaki Beef & Pea Pods

Chinese parsley, coriander and cilantro are all the same herb.

2 teaspoons cornstarch
2 tablespoons dry sherry

2 tablespoons soy sauce

1 tablespoon honey

¼ teaspoon grated gingerroot or ⅛ teaspoon ground ginger

8 ounces beef top sirloin steak, trimmed, thinly sliced across grain in 2-inch strips

8 Chinese pea pods

¼ cup slivered almonds

Cilantro (Chinese parsley or coriander) or fresh parsley

1 cup hot cooked rice

In a 1½-quart microwave-safe glass dish, combine cornstarch, sherry, soy sauce, honey and gingerroot or ginger. Microwave on 100% (HIGH) 1½ minutes, stirring once. Remove from oven. Stir in beef. Microwave on 100% (HIGH) 2 minutes, stirring once. Remove from oven. Stir in pea pods. Microwave on 100% (HIGH) 1 to 1½ minutes or until beef is no longer pink. Sprinkle with almonds; garnish with parsley or cilantro. Serve over rice. Makes 2 servings.

---

*Chef's Tip*

Cooking bags keep the oven clean. Close oven cooking bags with a piece of string or a strip of plastic. Paper-covered twister ties tend to heat up and melt the bags.

# *Microwaved Pot Roast*

You never thought of making pot roast in a microwave oven? Try it.

**2 tablespoons dry onion soup mix**
**½ cup beer**
**1 pound beef chuck roast**
**¼ teaspoon salt**
**¼ teaspoon paprika**
**¼ teaspoon pepper**

In a 1-quart microwave-safe casserole dish, mix onion soup and beer. Set aside. Sprinkle beef with salt, paprika and pepper. Place in dish. Cover tightly. Microwave on 50% (MEDIUM) 25 minutes, rotating dish halfway through cooking. Let stand 5 minutes. Makes 2 servings.

# Browning & Flavor Agents

## Browning Glaze

**2 tablespoons browning sauce**
**2 tablespoons water**

In a custard cup, combine browning sauce and water. Brush on all sides of meat before and during microwaving to enhance color and flavor.

## Browning & Seasoning Mix

**1 tablespoon salt**
**⅛ teaspoon garlic salt**
**¼ teaspoon dried parsley flakes**
**1 teaspoon paprika**
**⅛ teaspoon lemon pepper**

In a small bowl, combine salt, garlic salt, parsley flakes, paprika and lemon pepper. Sprinkle on all sides of meat before microwaving to enhance color and flavor.

**2 tablespoons butter or margarine**
**½ teaspoon paprika**
**2 drops liquid smoke**

In a custard cup, microwave butter or margarine, paprika and liquid smoke on 100% (HIGH) 1 minute or until butter or margarine melts; stir well.

# Rack of Lamb

Don't save this wonderful treat for special occasions only.

**1 (1¼ lb.) 8-rib rack of lamb,**
   **trimmed**
**1 tablespoon butter or margarine**
**½ cup dry bread crumbs**
**1 garlic clove, finely chopped**
**½ teaspoon finely chopped fresh**
   **mint**
**½ teaspoon finely chopped or**
   **crumbled fresh rosemary**

In a microwave-safe dish, lay lamb flat, bone side down. Set aside. In a small microwave-safe bowl, microwave butter or margarine on 100% (HIGH) 15 to 20 seconds or until melted. Remove from oven. Stir in bread crumbs, garlic, mint and rosemary. Pat crumb mixture over lamb, covering completely. Microwave on 100% (HIGH) 6 to 9 minutes or until a thermometer inserted in thickest part, not touching bone, registers 160F. Makes 2 servings.

# Lamb Curry

Add more curry for a stronger flavor.

**4 ounces boneless lamb, trimmed, cut in 1-inch cubes**
**¼ cup chopped onion**
**¼ cup chopped apple**
**1 tablespoon butter or margarine**
**1 tablespoon all-purpose flour**
**¼ teaspoon chicken bouillon granules**
**½ teaspoon curry powder**
**½ cup milk**
**½ cup hot cooked rice**
**Condiments: chutney, raisins, shredded unsweetened coconut, peanuts, chopped green onion**

Place lamb in a small microwave-safe dish. Cover tightly. Microwave on 100% (HIGH) 3 to 4 minutes or until lamb is no longer pink; stir. Set aside. In a small microwave-safe casserole dish, microwave onion, apple and butter or margarine on 100% (HIGH) 2 minutes. Remove from oven. Stir in flour, bouillon granules and curry powder. Microwave on 100% (HIGH) 30 seconds. Remove from oven. Gradually stir in milk, then lamb. Microwave on 100% 3 minutes or until mixture comes to a boil, stirring once. Serve over rice with assorted condiments. Makes 1 serving.

# Hungarian Pork Chops

Microwaving the pork chops tightly covered ensures the pork will be done.

- ¼ teaspoon paprika
- ¼ teaspoon salt
- ⅛ teaspoon pepper
- 2 (7-oz.) pork loin chops, ¾-inch thick
- 3 tablespoons ketchup

**1 tablespoon Dijon-style mustard**
**1 tablespoon Worcestershire sauce**
**½ cup dairy sour cream**
**½ avocado**

In a custard cup, combine paprika, salt and pepper. Sprinkle both sides of chops with seasonings. Place in a microwave-safe dish with meat toward outside of dish. Cover tightly. Microwave on 50% (MEDIUM) 6 minutes. Set aside. In a custard cup, mix ketchup, mustard and Worcestershire sauce. Pour over meat; re-cover. Microwave on 50% (MEDIUM) 6 minutes. Remove meat to a serving plate. Stir sour cream into liquid in cooking dish. Microwave on 100% (HIGH) 1½ to 2 minutes or just until warm. Pour over meat. Slice avocado; garnish pork chops with avocado. Makes 2 servings.

# *Apricot-Glazed Ham Steak*

Microwave right on your dinner plate!

**1 (4-oz.) ham steak**
**1 teaspoon apricot jam**

**1 teaspoon finely chopped green bell pepper**
**1 teaspoon raisins**
**2 canned apricot halves**

Place ham on a microwave-safe serving plate. Spread with apricot jam. Sprinkle with bell pepper and raisins; top with apricot halves. Cover tightly. Microwave on 100% (HIGH) 2 to 3 minutes or until heated through. Let stand, covered, 2 minutes. Makes 1 serving.

# Barbecued Country Ribs

Use hot pads when handling the dish; it gets hot from the ribs.

**1½ pounds country-style pork ribs, cut in serving pieces**
**½ cup water**
**¾ cup prepared chili sauce**
**¼ cup orange marmalade**
**1 tablespoon white wine vinegar**
**1 teaspoon Worcestershire sauce**

Place ribs in a microwave-safe dish. Add water. Cover tightly. Microwave on 50%

(MEDIUM) 10 minutes. Remove from oven. Turn ribs over; rearrange, moving outside ribs to center. Microwave on 50% (MEDIUM) 10 minutes more. Set aside. In a small bowl, combine chili sauce, marmalade, vinegar and Worcestershire sauce. Drain ribs. Pour sauce over ribs. Microwave on 50% (MEDIUM) 10 minutes. Makes 2 servings.

# Pork Chops with Cider Glaze

Pork chops are attractive and flavorful when paired with this shiny brown glaze.

**2 (6-oz.) pork loin chops**
**1 medium-size red cooking apple, cored, sliced in thin wedges**
**½ medium-size onion, thinly sliced**
**⅓ cup apple cider**
**½ teaspoon beef bouillon granules**
**½ teaspoon cornstarch**
**⅛ teaspoon ground sage**
**⅛ teaspoon dried leaf thyme**

Place meat on a microwave-safe plate. Cover tightly. Microwave on 100% (HIGH) 3 minutes. Remove from oven. Turn meat over; re-cover. Microwave on 100% (HIGH) 4 to 5 minutes more. Remove from oven; keep covered. Set aside. In a small microwave-safe bowl, place apple and onion. Cover tightly. Microwave on 100% (HIGH) 2 minutes. Set aside. In a small bowl, combine apple cider, bouillon granules, cornstarch, sage and thyme. Stir until cornstarch dissolves. Pour over apple and onion mixture. Microwave on 100% (HIGH) 3 to 4 minutes or until liquid comes to a boil and thickens slightly, stirring several times. Pour apple mixture over chops. If needed, microwave on 100% (HIGH) 2 minutes to reheat. Makes 2 servings.

# Pork "Stir Fry"

Cut celery, onion and carrot diagonally to expose more surface.

**8 ounces lean pork, thinly sliced across grain**
**½ cup broccoli flowerets, cut in 1-inch pieces**
**½ medium-size onion, thinly sliced**
**¼ cup thinly sliced carrot**

**6 fresh mushrooms, thinly sliced**
**8 Chinese pea pods**
**½ cup bean sprouts**
**2 tablespoons soy sauce**
**2 teaspoons sugar**
**¼ cup beef broth**
**¼ teaspoon cornstarch**

Place pork in a 1-quart microwave-safe casserole dish. Cover tightly. Microwave on 100% (HIGH) 2 minutes. Remove from oven. If needed, stir to break up pieces. Stir in broccoli, onion and carrot; re-cover. Microwave on 100% (HIGH) 2½ minutes. Remove from oven. Stir in mushrooms, pea pods and bean sprouts; re-cover. Set aside. In a custard cup, combine soy sauce, sugar, beef broth and cornstarch. Pour over meat and vegetables; re-cover. Microwave on 100% (HIGH) 3 minutes or until sauce thickens slightly, stirring several times. Let stand 3 minutes. Makes 2 servings.

---

*Chef's Tip*
Place thicker pieces of food toward outside of dish.

---

# POULTRY

Chicken and turkey are both popular and versatile. Sold by the piece or part—legs, thighs, breasts, wings—they play many roles: plain, pounded, rolled or cubed. Poultry has a mild taste that combines with a wide assortment of flavors—spicy Mexican seasoning, a sherry cream sauce, or just cooked with a sprig of fresh dill and a shake of lemon pepper.

You'll need six ounces of bone-in poultry per serving. For boneless cuts, you'll need four ounces per serving. Small Cornish game hens can serve one person, a large one two persons. When cooking pieces of poultry with the bone in, such as a leg, it may be necessary to shield the part where there is little meat by wrapping a small piece of foil around it to deflect microwaves and prevent overcooking.

If you like the elegant look of a whole bird for a festive occasion, try a Cornish game hen. Glaze with traditional Cranberry Sauce or coat with a Parmesan bread-crumb mixture and take along on a picnic.

Refrigerate poultry no longer than two days. If purchasing ahead of time, it freezes well and defrosts easily and quickly in a microwave oven. I often decide what I will eat just before I'm ready to eat, not hours earlier. Defrosting in a microwave oven gives you that option. You may want to microwave twice as much as needed and freeze the other half for another time. True, a microwave does cook fast, but preparation and cleanup time still have to be considered. It's a real treat to take a home-cooked meal out of your freezer and put it on a serving plate, defrost, microwave and be ready to eat in five minutes with only the plate to wash.

Skinning poultry removes many calories. The moist heat of microwave cooking keeps skinned poultry from drying out. Microwaved chicken and turkey pieces are tender and juicy, but for some they are bit a pale in appearance. If desired, many coatings, toppings and sauces can be used on poultry, with or without skin.

No special dishes are needed for microwaving poultry. Use ones large enough so poultry can be arranged in a single layer with room for easy turning. Most recipes instruct to cover tightly to keep heat and moisture in; this also allows food to cook more evenly. A rule of thumb for poultry is six minutes per pound on 100% (HIGH) for whole birds or legs and five minutes per pound on 100% (HIGH) for boneless pieces or breasts.

# Normandy Chicken

Calvados is a type of French apple brandy.

**2 (4-oz.) boneless skinned chicken breasts**
**2 tablespoons Calvados or apple brandy**
**½ cup apple cider**
**Pinch dried leaf thyme**
**Pinch dried leaf rosemary**
**2 tablespoons dairy sour cream**

Place chicken in a microwave-safe casserole dish. Pour brandy and cider over chicken. Sprinkle with thyme and rosemary. Cover tightly. Microwave on 100% (HIGH) 5 minutes or until chicken is no longer pink when cut. Remove chicken to serving plates. Stir sour cream into hot liquid in dish. Microwave on 100% (HIGH) 1 minute; do not boil. Pour over chicken. Makes 2 servings.

# Teriyaki Chicken

Remove chicken skin to reduce calories.

**2 (6-oz.) chicken breast halves or thighs**
**2 tablespoons ketchup**
**1 tablespoon soy sauce**
**2 teaspoons brown sugar**

Place chicken pieces in a small microwave-safe dish, bone side down and thickest part to outside of dish. In a custard cup, mix ketchup, soy sauce and brown sugar. Brush over chicken. Cover tightly. Microwave on 100% (HIGH) 4 minutes. Remove from oven. Baste chicken with sauce; re-cover. Microwave on 100% (HIGH) 2 to 3 minutes more or until chicken is no longer pink when cut. Uncover; let stand 5 minutes. Makes 2 servings.

# Bacon-Wrapped Chicken Wings

Serve as an entrée or an appetizer.

**4 chicken wings, disjointed**
**2 tablespoons soy sauce**
**2 tablespoons ketchup**
**1 tablespoon brown sugar**
**1 tablespoon dry sherry**
**2 drops sesame oil, if desired**
**1 small garlic clove, finely chopped**
**4 slices bacon, cut in half crosswise**

Discard wing tips. In a small bowl, mix soy sauce, ketchup, brown sugar, sherry, sesame oil if desired and garlic. Add chicken; stir to coat. Let stand 20 minutes. Remove chicken from sauce. Wrap with bacon. Secure with a wooden pick. Place in a microwave-safe dish. Cover tightly. Microwave on 100% (HIGH) 4 to 5 minutes or until bacon is crisp. Drain on a paper towel. Makes 2 servings.

# Spinach-Stuffed Chicken Breast

Loosen skin to form a pocket for stuffing.

**2 (4-oz.) boneless chicken breasts**
**1 (10-oz.) package frozen chopped spinach**
**2 tablespoons chopped onion**
**2 tablespoons shredded carrot**
**1 tablespoon grated Parmesan cheese**
**1 tablespoon butter or margarine**
**½ cup seasoned bread crumbs**
**⅛ teaspoon paprika**

Using a sharp knife, loosen skin on chicken by cutting membrane holding skin to meat; leave skin attached on 3 sides with opening large enough to hold stuffing. Set aside. Remove wrapper from spinach. Microwave on 50% (MEDIUM) 4 minutes or until thawed. Drain well. In a small bowl, combine spinach, onion, carrot and cheese. Gently push stuffing into pocket between skin and meat. Pat down skin to smooth. Place breasts, stuffing side up, in a microwave-safe dish. Set aside. In a small microwave-safe bowl, microwave butter or margarine on 100% (HIGH) 15 to 20 seconds or until melted. Stir in bread crumbs and paprika. Pat on chicken to evenly cover. Cover with wax paper. Microwave on 70% (MEDIUM-HIGH) 10 to 12 minutes or until chicken is no longer pink when cut. Makes 2 servings.

# Chicken Kiev

What fun to make party food easily, just for yourself!

**2 tablespoons firm butter or margarine**
**1 (4-oz.) boneless skinned chicken breast, pounded ¼-inch thick**
**⅛ teaspoon dried leaf tarragon**
**Seasoned salt**
**Paprika**

Place 1 tablespoon of butter or margarine at narrow end of chicken. Sprinkle with tarragon. Roll up, jelly-roll style, tucking in sides of chicken to completely enclose butter or margarine. Place in a small microwave-safe glass dish. Set aside. In a custard cup, microwave remaining butter or margarine on

100% (HIGH) 15 to 20 seconds or until melted. Brush over chicken. Sprinkle with seasoned salt and paprika. Cover tightly. Refrigerate at least 30 minutes or overnight. Microwave on 100% (HIGH) 2 minutes. Remove from oven. Turn chicken over; recover. Microwave on 100% (HIGH) 1 to 2 minutes more or until chicken turns from translucent to opaque. Let stand, covered, 5 minutes. Makes 1 serving.

# Chicken & Shrimp Kabobs

Bamboo skewers don't burn in a microwave oven.

¼ cup soy sauce
1 teaspoon sugar
1 teaspoon chopped fresh gingerroot
¼ teaspoon garlic salt
1 teaspoon lemon juice
2 tablespoons dry sherry
1 (4-oz.) boneless skinned chicken breast, cut in 1-inch cubes
6 large shrimp, peeled, deveined
½ green bell pepper, cut in 1-inch squares

In a 1-quart dish, mix soy sauce, sugar, gingerroot, garlic salt, lemon juice and sherry. Stir in chicken, shrimp and bell pepper. Cover tightly. Refrigerate 1 hour. Thread chicken, shrimp and bell pepper alternately on 2 wooden skewers. Reserve marinade. Place kabobs on a microwave-safe platter. Cover tightly. Microwave on 100% (HIGH) 3 minutes. Remove from oven. Brush with reserved marinade; re-cover. Microwave on 100% (HIGH) 1 to 2 minutes or until chicken turns from translucent to opaque and shrimp are pink. Makes 2 servings.

# Florentine Chicken Rolls

Blue cheese and fresh spinach are rolled inside chicken breasts.

**4 large fresh spinach leaves, rinsed**
**2 (4-oz.) boneless skinned chicken breasts, pounded ¼-inch thick**
**2 teaspoons crumbled blue cheese**
**2 tablespoons dry bread crumbs**
**⅛ teaspoon paprika**

½ teaspoon finely chopped fresh
  parsley
1 tablespoon butter or margarine

Lay 2 spinach leaves on each chicken breast. Place blue cheese in center. Roll up, jelly-roll style, tucking in sides. Secure with a wooden pick. Place in a small microwave-safe casserole dish. Set aside. In a custard cup, combine bread crumbs, paprika and parsley. Set aside. In a custard cup, microwave butter or margarine on 100% (HIGH) 15 to 20 seconds or until melted. Brush chicken rolls with butter or margarine. Sprinkle with crumb mixture. Microwave on 100% (HIGH) 4 to 5 minutes or until chicken turns from translucent to opaque. Makes 2 servings.

# Mushroom & Almond-Stuffed Chicken Rolls

These can be assembled hours ahead.

2 tablespoons chopped celery
2 fresh mushrooms, chopped

¼ cup dry cornbread stuffing mix

1 (1-oz.) slice cooked ham, coarsely diced

½ teaspoon chopped fresh parsley

1 teaspoon slivered almonds

¼ teaspoon dried leaf basil

⅛ teaspoon salt

1 tablespoon butter or margarine

2 (4-oz.) boneless skinned chicken breasts, pounded ¼-inch thick

1 tablespoon soy sauce

In a small bowl, combine celery, mushrooms, stuffing mix, ham, parsley, almonds, basil and salt. Set aside. In a custard cup, microwave butter or margarine on 100% (HIGH) 15 to 20 seconds or until melted. Toss butter or margarine with stuffing mixture. Spoon stuffing down center of chicken. Roll up, jelly-roll style, tucking in sides. Secure with a wooden pick. Place in a microwave-safe casserole dish. Brush with soy sauce. Cover tightly. Microwave on 100% (HIGH) 5 minutes or until chicken turns from translucent to opaque. Uncover; let stand 5 minutes. Makes 2 servings.

# Chicken with Pistachio Sauce

Pistachio nuts are a beautiful green and grow in abundance in California.

> **2 (4-oz.) boneless skinned chicken breasts**
> **⅓ cup orange juice**
> **1 teaspoon lemon juice**
> **⅛ teaspoon orange peel**
> **⅛ teaspoon lemon peel**
> **1 tablespoon sliced green onion**
> **2 tablespoons shelled chopped pistachio nuts**
> **1 cup hot cooked rice**

Place chicken in a small microwave-safe casserole dish. Pour orange and lemon juices over chicken. Sprinkle with orange and lemon peels, green onions and nuts. Cover tightly. Microwave on 100% (HIGH) 4 to 6 minutes or until chicken is no longer pink when cut. Let stand, covered, 5 minutes. Serve over rice. Makes 2 servings.

# Curried Chicken & Rice

Make a double batch and freeze one for later.

**2 tablespoons butter or margarine**
**1 tablespoon grated onion**
**1 cup cooked rice**
**¼ teaspoon curry powder**
**¼ teaspoon celery salt**
**Dash pepper**
**3 tablespoons chicken broth**
**1 tablespoon plain yogurt**
**1 cup bite-size cooked chicken**
**¼ cup raisins**
**2 tablespoons chopped salted**
  **peanuts**

In a small microwave-safe casserole dish, microwave butter or margarine on 100% (HIGH) 20 to 25 seconds or until melted. Remove from oven. Stir in onion. Microwave on 100% (HIGH) 30 seconds. Remove from oven. Stir in rice, curry powder, celery salt and pepper. Set aside. In a small bowl, combine broth and yogurt. Stir into rice mixture. Mix in chicken, raisins and peanuts.

Microwave on 100% (HIGH) 3 minutes or until heated through. Makes 1 serving.

# Turkey with Quick Béarnaise Sauce

Special enough for company and can be made in minutes!

> 1 (12-oz.) boneless turkey fillet
> 1 recipe Quick Béarnaise Sauce,
>     page 100
> 2 to 3 pitted black olives, chopped
> Fresh thyme

Place turkey in a microwave-safe plastic cooking bag. Close end of bag with a piece of plastic or a rubber band. Place bag in a microwave-safe glass or ceramic dish. Using tip of a sharp knife, pierce 2 to 3 steam-vent holes in top of bag. Microwave on 70% (MEDIUM-HIGH) 3 minutes. Remove from oven. Carefully turn turkey over within bag. (Do not turn bag over.) Microwave on 70% (MEDIUM-HIGH) 2 to 3 minutes more or until center of turkey is no longer pink when cut. Let stand, covered, 3 minutes.

Prepare Quick Béarnaise Sauce as directed. Slice turkey across grain in ½-inch slices. Top with sauce. Sprinkle with olives and thyme. Makes 2 servings.

# Soft Turkey Tacos

Soft tacos are made with warmed, not fried, tortillas.

**½ cup diced cooked turkey**
**¼ cup Salsa Frita, page 99**
**2 pimento-stuffed olives, sliced**
**4 (6-inch) corn tortillas**
**½ cup shredded lettuce**
**¼ cup (1-oz.) shredded Cheddar cheese**
**½ cup dairy sour cream**

In a small microwave-safe bowl, combine turkey, Salsa Frita and olives. Microwave on 100% (HIGH) 1 to 1½ minutes or until heated through. Set aside. In a plastic bag, microwave tortillas on 100% (HIGH) 5 to 10 seconds or until soft. Spoon turkey mixture on half of each tortilla. Top with lettuce, cheese and sour cream. Fold tortillas over to form semicircles. If needed, microwave tacos on 100% (HIGH) 15 seconds to reheat. Makes 2 servings.

---

*Chef's Tip*
To warm finger towels, place 2 dampened and folded finger towels on a microwave-safe plate. Microwave on 100% (HIGH) 60 seconds or until hot.

---

# Sweet & Sour Turkey

---

Turkey with an oriental flair!

**4 (3-oz.) turkey breast slices**
**¼ cup Chablis wine**
**¼ cup ketchup**
**¼ cup apricot jam**
**¼ cup crushed pineapple**
**1 cup hot cooked rice**

Place turkey in a medium-size microwave-safe casserole dish. Pour wine over turkey. Cover tightly. Microwave on 100% (HIGH) 3 minutes or until turkey is no longer pink. Set aside. To make sauce, in a 1-cup glass measure, combine ketchup, jam and pineapple. Microwave on 100% (HIGH) 3 minutes. Stir; set aside. Drain turkey. Arrange turkey on rice. Top with sauce. Makes 2 servings.

# Dijon Cornish Hen

Most Cornish hens now are large enough to serve 2 people.

**1 (22-oz.) Cornish game hen, thawed if frozen, giblets removed**
**¼ cup Dijon-style mustard**
**⅓ cup dry bread crumbs**
**1 tablespoon finely chopped fresh parsley**

Place hen on a microwave-safe rack set in a microwave-safe dish. Brush entire hen with mustard. In a small bowl, combine bread crumbs and parsley. Pat on hen, covering completely. Cover loosely. Microwave on 70% (MEDIUM-HIGH) 10 to 12 minutes or until juices run clear when hen is cut between breast and thigh, rotating dish after 5 minutes. Uncover; let stand 5 minutes. To serve, cut in half or carve. Makes 2 servings.

*Chef's Tip*

If your microwave oven has only 1 or 2 speeds, setting a 1-cup glass measure full of water in the oven with food to be micro-waved will slow the cooking process.

# SEAFOOD

Seafood has become one of Americas most important "catches". It has wonderful nutritional value in addition to good flavor, versatility and speedy ease of preparation—a perfect subject for microwave cooking. When prepared in a microwave oven, seafood retains its natural moisture, delicate flavor and texture. Seafood is sold in various portion sizes so it works well in recipes that serve one or two people.

The microwave quickly poaches, steams or bakes fish. Fish may be prepared simply with butter or margarine, salt and pepper, or with wine, broth, sauce or vegetables. To microwave, allow four to six minutes per pound on 100% (HIGH). Thick pieces of fish or additional ingredients will lengthen the cooking time. Halfway through the cooking period, rotate the dish one-fourth turn and continue to microwave for the minimum recommended cooking time. Except for breaded fish sticks or fillets, let stand, covered, after cooking.

*General guidelines for
cooking fish and shellfish:*

**Fish fillets**—Place in a microwave-safe glass dish with the thickest parts of fish toward the outside. Cover tightly or cover with wax paper. Microwave on 100% (HIGH) four to six minutes per pound. Fish should flake, but be slightly undercooked in the thickest part.

**Roulades**—Rolled fish fillets can be a classic masterpiece. Place fish rolls, seam-side down, in a circular pattern in a microwave-safe glass dish. Add a small amount of liquid, if desired. Cover tightly. Microwave on 100% (HIGH) five to eight minutes per pound. Roulades should flake easily. A sauce may be prepared in the microwave oven with remaining juice.

**Steaks**—Line a microwave-safe glass dish with a paper towel to absorb juice, if desired. Arrange thicker pieces of fish, such as salmon or halibut, with narrow ends toward the center or in an alternating pattern. Allow space between steaks. Cover tightly. Microwave on 100% (HIGH) five to six minutes

144

per pound. Halfway through the cooking period, turn fish over if possible.

**Whole fish**—Place a whole fish in a microwave-safe glass dish. If preparing more than one fish, place the thickest parts toward the outside. Brush with lemon butter for a "poached" appearance or with a browning sauce for a "baked" appearance. Cover tightly or cover with wax paper. Microwave on 100% (HIGH) six to eight minutes per pound.

**Shellfish in the shell**—A microwave oven can be used to easily open shells of oysters or clams. Place scrubbed shells, in a circle, in a microwave-safe dish. Cover tightly. Microwave on 100% (HIGH) one to two minutes. To eat raw, remove shells from dish as soon as they open. If oyster meat is to be cooked, it should be pierced with a fork after the shell opens or it might burst with further microwaving.

**Breaded fillets or fish sticks**—Separate and arrange fish in a microwave-safe glass dish. For a drier texture, place fish on a microwave-safe rack. If fish is frozen, there is no need to defrost before microwaving. Microwave on 100% (HIGH) four to five minutes per pound. Fish should flake easily when done.

**Frozen packaged fillets and steaks**—To defrost, place package in microwave oven. Microwave half of the estimated time to defrost. Flex package; if not pliable, return to microwave oven. Rotate package and continue to microwave the total minimum time for defrosting. When package is pliable, open and separate pieces. Arrange in a microwave-safe glass dish with the least-defrosted pieces on top and outside. Continue to microwave only as needed. Fish should be slightly icy.

For best flavor and texture, thicker pieces or whole fish should be defrosted prior to preparation. Generally allow two to three minutes per pound on 100% (HIGH), or six to ten minutes per pound on 30% (MEDIUM-LOW). Let stand five to ten minutes. Thin pieces of fish (or thin packages) will require less time to defrost than thick pieces of fish (or thick packages).

# Sweet 'n' Sour Swordfish

If desired, substitute chicken for swordfish.

**½ (8-oz.) can pineapple chunks in pineapple juice**
**1 cup broccoli flowerets**
**4 water chestnuts, thinly sliced**
**¼ red bell pepper, thinly sliced**
**1 (10-oz.) swordfish steak, boned, cut in 1-inch chunks**
**1 tablespoon brown sugar**
**3 tablespoons ketchup**
**1 tablespoon white wine vinegar**
**1 teaspoon cornstarch**
**1 tablespoon sliced almonds**
**1 tablespoon sliced green onion**

Drain pineapple; reserve 2 tablespoons juice. In a medium-size microwave-safe casserole dish, combine pineapple, broccoli, water chestnuts and bell pepper. Cover tightly. Microwave on 100% (HIGH) 1 minute. Stir in swordfish. Set aside. In a small bowl, combine reserved pineapple juice, brown sugar, ketchup, vinegar and cornstarch. Stir until cornstarch dissolves. Stir into vegetables and swordfish to coat evenly. Cover tightly. Microwave on 100% (HIGH) 2 to 3 minutes or until swordfish is opaque and vegetables are tender-crisp. Let stand, covered, 3 minutes. Sprinkle with almonds and green onion. Makes 2 servings.

# Shrimp-Sauced Sole

Serve with a fresh green salad and crusty French bread.

> **2 tablespoons chopped celery**
> **2 tablespoons butter or margarine**
> **2 tablespoons all-purpose flour**
> **½ teaspoon chopped fresh dill**
> **¾ cup milk**
> **2 teaspoons Dijon-style mustard**
> **4 ounces small bay shrimp**
> **Dash hot-pepper sauce**
> **12 ounces sole fillets**

To make sauce, in a small microwave-safe bowl, microwave celery and butter or margarine on 100% (HIGH) 1½ to 2 minutes or until celery is tender. Remove from oven. Stir in flour and dill. Microwave on 100% (HIGH) 30 seconds. Remove from oven. Gradually stir in milk and mustard. Microwave on 100%

(HIGH) 2 to 3 minutes or until mixture comes to a boil, stirring several times. Stir in shrimp and hot-pepper sauce. Set aside. Place fillets in a microwave-safe casserole dish. Cover tightly. Microwave on 100% (HIGH) 3 to 5 minutes or until opaque. If needed, microwave sauce on 100% (HIGH) 1 minute to reheat. To serve, drain fillets; pour sauce over fillets. Makes 2 servings.

# Sole Papillon

Serve with tender zucchini slices.

**1 tablespoon butter or margarine**
**4 medium-size fresh mushrooms, thinly sliced**
**½ cup whipping cream**
**2 teaspoons all-purpose flour**
**1 tablespoon dry white wine**
**2 tablespoons grated carrot**
**2 (4-oz.) sole fillets**
**2 small fresh dill sprigs**
**2 (10-inch) squares parchment paper**

Place butter or margarine and mushrooms in a small microwave-safe bowl. Cover tightly. Microwave on 100% (HIGH) 1 minute. Remove from oven. Set aside. In a small bowl, whisk cream and flour. Stir into mushroom mixture. Microwave on 100% (HIGH) 2 to 2½ minutes or until mixture comes to a boil. Remove from oven. Stir in wine and carrot. Microwave on 100% (HIGH) 1 minute. Set aside. Fold each piece of paper in half to form a triangle, then open flat. Place a fillet on ½ of each piece of paper. Spoon cream mixture over fillets. Top with dill sprigs. Fold other ½ of paper over fillets. Fold edges of paper over 2 to 3 times to completely seal. On a large microwave-safe plate, microwave packets on 100% (HIGH) 2 to 3 minutes. Let stand 3 minutes. To serve, cut an "X" in top of each. Makes 2 servings.

# *Salmon Florentine*

Spinach is believed to have originated in Persia, which is where most children wished it had stayed!

**1 bunch fresh spinach, rinsed, trimmed**
**2 (5- to 6-oz.) salmon steaks or fillets**
**1 recipe Tarragon-Mustard Sauce, page 100**

Tear larger spinach leaves in bite-size pieces. Arrange in an 8-inch-square microwave-safe dish. Place salmon on top of spinach. Cover tightly. Microwave on 100% (HIGH) 3½ to 4 minutes or until salmon is opaque. Let stand, covered, 3 minutes. Prepare Tarragon-Mustard Sauce as directed. Spoon over salmon. Makes 2 servings.

# Salmon with Black Caviar

Fresh broccoli and a green salad complete this meal!

**2 (6- to 8-oz.) salmon steaks**
**3 tablespoons dry white wine**
**¼ cup butter or margarine**
**1 tablespoon thinly sliced green onion**
**1 teaspoon black lumpfish caviar**

Place salmon in a microwave-safe casserole dish. Sprinkle with 2 tablespoons of wine. Cover tightly. Microwave on 100% (HIGH) 3 to 5 minutes or until opaque. Set aside. In a 1-cup glass measure, microwave butter or margarine, green onion and remaining wine on 100% (HIGH) 1 minute or until butter or margarine is completely melted. Stir in caviar. Pour sauce over salmon. Makes 2 servings.

# Mushroom-Topped Halibut Steaks

Swordfish, snapper or sea bass can be substituted for halibut.

2 (6-oz.) halibut steaks, about ¾-inch thick
1 tablespoon lemon juice
¼ teaspoon dried leaf oregano
4 ounces fresh mushrooms, thinly sliced
1 tablespoon dry white wine
1 tablespoon thinly sliced green onion

Place halibut in a microwave-safe casserole dish. Sprinkle with lemon juice and oregano. Cover tightly. Set aside. In a small microwave-safe bowl, combine mushrooms, wine and green onion. Cover tightly. Microwave on 100% (HIGH) 1½ minutes. Uncover; set aside. Microwave halibut on 100% (HIGH) 3 to 4 minutes or until opaque. Let stand 5 minutes. Transfer halibut to serving plates. If needed, microwave mushroom mixture on 100% (HIGH) 30 seconds to reheat. Spoon mushroom mixture over halibut. Makes 2 servings.

# Mediterranean Halibut

This dish is as colorful as it is good.

**½ medium-size onion, thinly sliced**
**1 garlic clove, minced**
**1 tablespoon butter or margarine**
**1 small green zucchini, thinly sliced**
**1 small yellow zucchini or crookneck squash, thinly sliced**
**6 pitted ripe olives, chopped**
**1 medium-size tomato, chopped**
**½ teaspoon dried leaf oregano**
**2 (6-oz.) halibut fillets**

In a 1½ quart microwave-safe casserole dish, place onion, garlic and butter or margarine. Cover tightly. Microwave on 100% (HIGH)

3 minutes. Remove from oven. Stir in squash, olives, tomato and oregano; re-cover. Microwave on 100% (HIGH) 5 to 6 minutes or until squash is tender-crisp. Remove from oven. Place fillets on top of vegetables; re-cover. Microwave on 100% (HIGH) 3 to 4 minutes or until fillets are opaque. Makes 2 servings.

# *Halibut Stroganoff*

Classic stroganoff flavor with an up-to-date variation!

1 tablespoon butter or margarine
1 (6- to 8-oz.) halibut fillet, cut in ¼-inch-thick strips
¼ medium-size onion, sliced
4 medium-size fresh mushrooms, sliced
1 tablespoon dry white wine
1 teaspoon lemon juice
¼ teaspoon salt
¼ teaspoon Worcestershire sauce
1 teaspoon Dijon-style mustard
Dash pepper
½ cup dairy sour cream
1 cup hot cooked brown rice
1 teaspoon chopped fresh parsley

In a medium-size microwave-safe casserole dish, microwave butter or margarine on 100% (HIGH) 15 to 20 seconds. Remove from oven. Stir in halibut, onion, mushrooms, wine, lemon juice, salt, Worcestershire sauce, mustard and pepper. Microwave on 100% (HIGH) 4 minutes or until halibut is opaque, stirring once. Remove from oven. Stir in sour cream. Microwave on 100% (HIGH) 1 minute; do not boil. Spoon over rice. Sprinkle with parsley. Makes 1 or 2 servings.

# Stuffed Trout Amandine

An elegant presentation!

¼ **cup butter or margarine**
¾ **cup dry cornbread stuffing mix**
**2 tablespoons finely chopped onion**
**2 tablespoons finely chopped fresh parsley**
**2 (8-oz.) mountain trout**
**Seasoned salt**
**Juice 1 lemon**
½ **to** ⅓ **cup sliced toasted almonds**
**Fresh dill, if desired**
**Lemon wedges, if desired**

In a small microwave-safe bowl, microwave butter or margarine on 100% (HIGH) 45 seconds to 1 minute or until melted. Stir in stuffing mix, onion and parsley. Set aside. Sprinkle skin and inside of trout with seasoned salt. Spoon cornbread mixture into cavities of trout. Tuck almonds inside trout. Place in a microwave-safe serving dish. Sprinkle lemon juice over trout. Cover tightly. Microwave on 100% (HIGH) 6 to 8 minutes or until trout flakes easily. Let stand, covered, 3 minutes. Garnish with dill and lemon wedges, if desired. Makes 2 servings.

# Mountain Trout

Fresh or frozen trout are available almost year-round.

> 1 (8-oz.) mountain trout
> 1 tablespoon butter or margarine
> 2 teaspoons lemon juice
> 1 sprig fresh cilantro (Chinese parsley or coriander)
> 1 tablespoon finely chopped green onion

Place trout in a microwave-safe dish. Set aside. In a custard cup, microwave butter or margarine and lemon juice on 100% (HIGH) 15 to 20 seconds or until butter or margarine melts. Brush mixture on both sides and inside cavity of trout. Fill cavity with cilantro and green onion. Cover tightly. Microwave on 100% (HIGH) 2 to 3 minutes or until trout flakes easily. Let stand, covered, 3 minutes. Makes 1 serving.

# *Crispy Cod Fillets*

This coating tastes great on chicken, too.

½ cup corn flake crumbs
1 tablespoon grated Parmesan
   cheese
1 tablespoon chopped green onion
   stem
¼ teaspoon paprika
2 (6-oz.) cod fillets
1 egg, beaten

In a pie plate, combine corn flake crumbs, cheese, green onion stem and paprika. Dip each fillet in egg. Cover completely with crumbs. On a microwave-safe rack set in a microwave-safe dish, microwave on 100% (HIGH) 3 to 4 minutes or until fillets flake easily. Makes 2 servings.

# Coquilles St. Jacques

Substitute crab for scallops next time.

**1 tablespoon butter or margarine**
**1 green onion, thinly sliced**
**1 tablespoon all-purpose flour**
**½ cup milk or half and half**
**Dash hot-pepper sauce**
**⅛ teaspoon salt**
**1 tablespoon dry white wine**
**8 ounces scallops**
**3 medium-size fresh mushrooms,**
  **thinly sliced**
**1 teaspoon finely chopped fresh**
  **parsley**

In a microwave-safe casserole dish, micro-wave butter or margarine and onion on 100% (HIGH) 15 to 20 seconds or until butter or margarine melts. Remove from oven. Stir in flour. Microwave on 100% (HIGH) 15 seconds. Remove from oven. Stir in milk or half and half. Microwave on 100% (HIGH) 2½ to 3 minutes or until mixture starts to thicken, stirring once. Remove from oven. Stir in hot-pepper sauce, salt, wine, scallops and mush-rooms. Microwave on 100% (HIGH) 1½ to 2 minutes or until scallops are opaque, stirring once. Spoon mixture into 2 microwave-safe ramekins. Sprinkle with parsley. If needed, microwave on 100% (HIGH) 1 minute to reheat. Makes 2 servings.

---

*Chef's Tip*
Having another appliance on the same electrical circuit or using an extension cord will cause a microwave oven to lose some power and foods will take longer to cook.

---

# Bacon-Scallops Sauté

The ultimate for scallop lovers! Use large sea scallops, if available.

**1 slice bacon, cut in ½-inch pieces**
**2 green onions, thinly sliced**
**10 ounces sea scallops**
**Juice ½ lemon**

Place bacon and green onions in a small microwave-safe casserole dish. Cover with a paper towel. Microwave on 100% (HIGH) 1½ minutes. Remove from oven. Stir to break up bacon. Mix in scallops and lemon juice. Microwave on 100% (HIGH) 1 to 2 minutes or until scallops are opaque. Makes 2 servings.

# *Steamers*

No need to go out to your favorite seafood restaurant—have steamers at home!

**12 small (littleneck) clams, shells scrubbed**
**½ cup clam juice**
**2 tablespoons butter or margarine**

Place clams flat in a single layer in a microwave-safe casserole dish. Pour clam juice over clams. Cover tightly. Microwave on 100% (HIGH) 2 to 4 minutes or just until all clams open. Discard any that do not open. In a small microwave-safe bowl, microwave butter or margarine 20 to 25 seconds or until melted. Serve butter or margarine for dipping clams. Drink clam juice after eating clams, if desired. Makes 1 or 2 servings.

# Clam Sauce with Tomatoes for Linguini

Linguini is traditional, but if you have only spaghetti on hand, use it.

1 (6½-oz.) can minced clams
1 green onion, finely chopped
1 medium-size tomato, seeded, chopped
1 garlic clove, minced
¼ cup olive oil
¼ teaspoon dried leaf oregano
3 tablespoons butter or margarine
⅓ cup dry white wine
2 tablespoons minced fresh parsley
2 cups hot cooked linguini, drained

Drain clam juice into a small microwave-safe casserole dish; reserve clams. Stir green onion, tomato, garlic, olive oil, oregano, butter or margarine and wine into clam juice. Microwave on 100% (HIGH) 4 minutes. Remove from oven. Stir in reserved clams and parsley. Microwave on 100% (HIGH) 1½ to 2 minutes or until clams are hot. Serve over linguini. Makes 2 servings.

# Oysters on the Half Shell

A plate of oysters and a glass of champagne make a perfect combination!

**6 oysters, shells scrubbed**
**Condiments: cocktail sauce,**
**Worcestershire sauce, prepared**
**horseradish, hot-pepper sauce**

In a microwave-safe casserole dish, arrange oysters in a cartwheel pattern with hinges pointing outward. Cover tightly. Microwave on 100% (HIGH) 1½ minutes or until shells open. Remove oysters as they open to avoid overcooking. Discard any that do not open. Cut oysters at muscle to separate from shell. Remove oysters from shells. Place an oyster in each top-rounded shell. Serve on a bed of crushed ice with assorted condiments. Makes 1 or 2 servings.

# Seafood Scampi

Scampi are a very large shrimp.

**2 tablespoons butter or margarine**
**1 tablespoon all-purpose flour**
**1 tablespoon lemon juice**
**1 tablespoon dry white wine**
**⅛ teaspoon garlic powder**
**1 teaspoon chopped fresh dill**
**6 scampi, peeled, deveined**
**4 ounces halibut, boned, cubed**
**6 ounces sea scallops**
**6 small (littleneck) clams, shells scrubbed**

In a 1-quart microwave-safe casserole dish, microwave butter or margarine on 100% (HIGH) 20 to 25 seconds or until melted. Remove from oven. Whisk in flour, then lemon juice, wine, garlic powder and dill. Add scampi, halibut and scallops; stir to coat. Place clams among seafood. Cover tightly. Microwave on 100% (HIGH) 4 to 5 minutes or until halibut and scallops are opaque and clams open. Discard any clams that do not open. Let stand, covered, 2 minutes. Makes 2 servings.

# Cioppino

Serve lots of crusty sourdough bread to soak up every last bit of sauce.

1 teaspoon olive oil
1 small tomato, seeded, finely chopped
¼ cup finely chopped onion
1 small garlic clove, minced
2 cups chicken broth
¼ cup dry white wine
⅛ teaspoon dried leaf rosemary
⅛ teaspoon dried leaf oregano
⅛ teaspoon dried leaf basil
1 (16-oz.) Dungeness crab, cleaned, cracked
4 clams, shells scrubbed
8 medium-size raw shrimp, peeled, deveined
4 ounces scallops

In a large microwave-safe casserole dish, combine olive oil, tomato, onion and garlic. Microwave on 100% (HIGH) 1 minute. Remove from oven. Stir in chicken broth, wine, rosemary, oregano and basil. Microwave on 100% (HIGH) 5 to 6 minutes or until mixture comes to a boil. Remove from oven. If desired, break crab in pieces. Add crab, clams, shrimp and scallops. Cover tightly. Microwave on 100% (HIGH) 5 minutes or until clams open and shrimp turns pink. Discard any clams that do not open. Makes 1 or 2 servings.

# VEGETABLES

"Colorful", "crisp" and "fresh-tasting" are descriptive words that come to mind when I think of microwaved vegetables. I could write an entire microwave cookbook just on vegetables! Cooking one artichoke conventionally with boiling water takes about thirty minutes compared to six minutes in a microwave oven. Wrap one ear of corn in plastic wrap, enclose a pat of butter or margarine and three minutes later you're ready to eat buttered corn. It's fantastic!

I recommend tightly covering all vegetables except baking potatoes. Tightly covering fresh, frozen or canned vegetables keeps moisture in and shortens cooking time. Because of the tight covering, vegetables will continue to cook, if left covered, when removed from a microwave oven. Be careful not to overcook. Vegetables that have a lot of natural moisture, such as corn, potatoes and tomatoes, need no added moisture. I always microwave vegetables on 100% (HIGH). Pierce vegetables that have a thick skin and are cooked whole, such as potatoes and acorn squash, to let steam escape so they don't explode while microwaving.

Many frozen vegetable packages now have microwave cooking directions. I feel most frozen vegetables are of very good quality and come in handy when fresh ones are out of season. Because most frozen vegetables are packaged in amounts too large for one or two servings, I usually remove the portion I need, then reseal the package and return it to the freezer for future use. Frozen packaged vegetables are also a good option for fresh vegetables, such as cauliflower, that are only sold whole. Consider, too, your saving in time—especially with fresh beans, peas and corn—as cleaning and preparation are already done.

Vegetables don't always have to be served hot. Microwave a double serving of green beans; eat half now and refrigerate the rest. For another meal, toss the cold beans with chopped tomato, slivered almonds and Italian salad dressing.

For a different fresh flavor, tuck a sprig of fresh herb, such as basil or oregano, into the vegetables. A small piece of lemon or orange peel can impart a fresh taste, especially to frozen or canned vegetables.

Carving vegetables in interesting shapes before microwaving is easy with only one or two servings. Cut carrots in flowers. Tie green beans with pieces of green onion stems. Use vegetables for serving cups—halve a bell pepper, hollow out a squash or a two-inch length of cucumber and fill with peas. A whole cooked artichoke with the choke removed makes a great "casserole dish."

It's fun to serve an assortment of vegetables arranged attractively and microwaved on a serving plate. Use lots of color—tomatoes, crookneck squash, beets, asparagus and Chinese pea pods. Cover tightly. Microwave six minutes per pound on 100% (HIGH). Let stand, covered, three minutes.

# Beets Amandine

A colorful and interesting dish.

**¾ teaspoon cornstarch**
**2 tablespoons brown sugar**
**¼ cup orange juice**
**2 teaspoons butter or margarine**
**1 (8¼-oz.) can sliced beets, drained**
**1 tablespoon slivered almonds**

In a 1-cup glass measure, combine corn-starch and brown sugar. Stir in orange juice. Add butter or margarine. Microwave on 100% (HIGH) 1½ minutes or until slightly thickened, stirring every 30 seconds. Set aside. Place beets in a small microwave-safe casserole dish. Pour sauce over beets. Sprinkle with almonds. Cover tightly. Microwave on 100% (HIGH) 1 minute. Makes 2 servings.

# Fresh Steamed Beets

Leave beet tops on if you like good-tasting greens. Beets peel easily after microwaving.

**1 pound small fresh beets, pierced**
**2 tablespoons water**

Place beets and water in a microwave-safe casserole dish. Cover tightly. Microwave on 100% (HIGH) 6 to 7 minutes or until beets are tender. Let stand, covered, 5 minutes. Peel. Makes 2 servings.

# Aunt Rose's Pickled Beets

These were always on the table at Aunt Rose's house.

> 1 (8¼-oz.) can sliced or small whole beets
> 2 tablespoons white vinegar
> 2 tablespoons sugar
> 1 (1-inch) piece cinnamon stick
> 2 whole cloves

In a small microwave-safe bowl, combine beets with juice, vinegar, sugar, cinnamon stick and cloves. Cover tightly. Microwave on 100% (HIGH) 2 minutes. Stir until sugar dissolves. Cool before serving. Remove cinnamon stick and cloves. Cover and refrigerate any leftover beets. Makes 2 servings.

# Susan's Artichoke

Serve melted butter or margarine or mayonnaise for dipping artichoke leaves.

**1 (10- to 12-oz.) artichoke**
**6 slices lemon, cut in halves**

Slice off top 1-inch of artichoke so top is flat. Using scissors, snip off point from each leaf. Rinse under cool water. Drain, but do not shake off all water. Tuck lemon into leaves. Wrap completely in plastic wrap. Place artichoke upside down in microwave oven. Microwave on 100% (HIGH) 5 to 7 minutes or until heart is tender when pierced from bottom. Remove from oven. Let stand, wrapped, 5 minutes. Serve warm or chilled. Makes 1 serving.

**To Make 2 Servings:**
Double recipe. Microwave on 100% (HIGH) 7 to 9 minutes. Let stand 5 minutes.

# Romanoff Potato

A potato fit for a king!

**1 (5-oz.) baking potato, pierced**
**¼ cup dairy sour cream**
**1 green onion, sliced**
**¼ cup (1-oz.) shredded Cheddar**
  **cheese**
**Black caviar, if desired**

Place potato in microwave oven. Microwave on 100% (HIGH) 3 minutes. Turn potato over. Microwave on 100% (HIGH) 1 to 3 minutes more or until potato gives slightly when squeezed. Wrap in foil. Let stand 5 minutes. Cut off top ⅓ of potato lengthwise. Carefully scoop out pulp into a small bowl. Combine sour cream, green onion and ½ of cheese with potato pulp. Spoon mixture back into shell. Sprinkle with remaining cheese. Microwave on 100% (HIGH) 45 seconds or until heated through. Top with caviar, if desired. Makes 1 serving.

# Chili-Cheese Potato

What a delicious way to prepare a potato!

**1 (5-oz.) baking potato, pierced**
**2 tablespoons milk**
**2 tablespoons dairy sour cream**
**1 teaspoon chopped green chilies**
**1 tablespoon shredded Cheddar cheese**

Place potato in microwave oven. Microwave on 100% (HIGH) 3 minutes. Turn potato over. Microwave on 100% (HIGH) 1 to 3 minutes more or until potato gives slightly when squeezed. Wrap in foil. Let stand 5 minutes. Cut a slice from top of potato. Carefully scoop out pulp into a small bowl. Add milk; mash. Stir in sour cream, green chilies and cheese. Spoon mixture back into shell. On a microwave-safe plate, microwave potato on 100% (HIGH) 1½ to 2 minutes or until heated through. Makes 1 serving.

*Chef's Tip*
The amount of electricity consumed by a microwave oven is similar to that used by an electric frying pan.

# Duchess Sweet Potatoes

If desired, prepare ahead and refrigerate. Microwave on 100% (HIGH) 2 minutes per serving.

**1 (16-oz.) can sweet potatoes or yams, drained, mashed**
**2 tablespoons orange juice**
**½ teaspoon grated orange peel**
**1 egg yolk**
**⅛ teaspoon ground cinnamon**
**Pinch ground nutmeg**

Using an electric mixer, in a medium-size bowl, mix sweet potatoes or yams, orange juice, orange peel, egg yolk, cinnamon and nutmeg until smooth. Spoon mixture into a pastry bag fitted with a large star tip. Pipe mixture around edges of 2 microwave-safe serving plates or in swirly mounds. Microwave each on 100% (HIGH) 1½ minutes. Makes 2 servings.

# *Parmesan Potatoes*

Parmesan cheese takes on a nut-like flavor when cooked.

**2 (5-oz.) baking potatoes, cut crosswise in ⅜-inch-thick slices**
**2 tablespoons butter or margarine**
**3 tablespoons grated Parmesan cheese**
**1 tablespoon fine dry bread crumbs**
**⅛ teaspoon garlic salt**

Arrange potatoes in a single layer on a microwave-safe plate or in a shallow microwave-safe dish. Set aside. In a custard cup, microwave butter or margarine on 100% (HIGH) 20 to 30 seconds or until melted. Brush on potatoes. Set aside. In a small bowl, combine cheese, bread crumbs and garlic salt. Sprinkle over potatoes. Cover tightly. Microwave on 100% (HIGH) 5 to 6 minutes or until potatoes are tender-crisp. Let stand, covered, 5 minutes. Makes 2 servings.

# Sweet Potato Surprises

A marshmallow is hidden in the center!

- **1 (16-oz.) can sweet potatoes or yams, drained**
- **1 tablespoon crushed pineapple, drained**
- **¼ teaspoon grated orange peel**
- **1 tablespoon orange juice**
- **2 large marshmallows**

In a small bowl, mash sweet potatoes or yams. Stir in pineapple, orange peel and juice. Fill 2 (¾-cup) microwave-safe ramekins ¼ full of potato mixture. Place marshmallows in center. Fill with remaining potato mixture, covering marshmallows completely. Cover loosely. Microwave on 100% (HIGH) 3 to 4 minutes or until heated through. Makes 2 servings.

# Tomato-Broccoli Toss

Bright red and green make this dish stand out on any plate.

- **1 medium-size tomato, cut in 8 wedges**

**1 cup broccoli flowerets**
**2 tablespoons shredded Monterey Jack cheese**

In a small microwave-safe casserole dish, toss tomato and broccoli. Sprinkle with cheese. Cover tightly. Microwave on 100% (HIGH) 2 to 2½ minutes or until broccoli is tender-crisp. Let stand, covered, 3 minutes. Makes 2 servings.

# Greek Tomatoes

Mint and feta cheese make these tomatoes something special!

**5 cherry tomatoes, pierced**
**1 tablespoon butter or margarine**
**½ teaspoon chopped fresh mint**
**1 tablespoon crumbled feta cheese**

In a small microwave-safe casserole dish, place tomatoes, butter or margarine and mint. Cover tightly. Microwave on 100% (HIGH) 1 minute. Shake dish to coat tomatoes with butter mixture. Microwave on 100% (HIGH) 30 seconds to 1 minute more or until tomatoes are hot but still retain shape. Let stand, covered, 3 minutes. Sprinkle with cheese. Makes 1 serving.

# *Insalata Caldo*

Serve as a vegetable dish or a hot tomato salad.

**2 (½-inch-thick) slices large tomato**
**1 (½-inch-thick) slice mozzarella**
**  cheese**
**1 teaspoon olive oil**
**¼ teaspoon dried leaf basil**
**1 teaspoon pine nuts**

On a microwave-safe plate, alternate tomato and cheese, overlapping slightly. Sprinkle with olive oil, basil and nuts. Cover tightly. Microwave on 100% (HIGH) 1 to 2 minutes or just until tomatoes are warm and cheese starts to melt. Let stand, covered, 3 minutes. Makes 1 serving.

# Oriental Eggplant in Tomato Shells

A unique way to serve eggplant.

**1 tablespoon soy sauce**
**1 teaspoon olive oil**
**¼ teaspoon sesame oil, if desired**
**1 Japanese eggplant or ¼ regular eggplant, peeled, cubed (about 6 ounces)**
**2 teaspoons chopped fresh cilantro (Chinese parsley or coriander)**
**1 large tomato, cut in half crosswise, pulp removed**

In a 1½ quart microwave-safe casserole dish, mix soy sauce, olive oil, and sesame oil, if desired. Toss eggplant and cilantro in soy sauce mixture. Cover tightly. Microwave on 100% (HIGH) 4 to 5 minutes or until eggplant is tender, stirring after 3 minutes. Spoon into tomato halves. Makes 2 servings.

# Zucchini & Tomatoes

A colorful presentation!

> 1 medium-size zucchini, thinly sliced
> ¼ teaspoon dried leaf basil
> 2 (½-inch-thick) tomato slices
> 1 tablespoon shredded Cheddar
>   cheese

Place zucchini and basil in a small microwave-safe bowl. Cover tightly. Microwave on 100% (HIGH) 2½ minutes or until tender. Set aside. Place tomato slices on a microwave-safe serving plate. Mound zucchini on tomatoes. Sprinkle with cheese. Cover tightly. Microwave on 100% (HIGH) 1½ minutes or until tomato is hot and cheese is melted. Makes 2 servings.

# Dill-Sauced Zucchini

Elegantly simple.

> 1 tablespoon butter or margarine
> 1 tablespoon beef broth
> 2 tablespoons half and half

184

1 tablespoon finely chopped fresh
   dill
2 medium-size zucchini, cut in
   julienne strips

In a medium-size microwave-safe serving
bowl, microwave butter or margarine on
100% (HIGH) 15 seconds or until melted.
Remove from oven. Stir in beef broth, half
and half and dill. Add zucchini; toss to coat
with sauce. Cover tightly. Microwave on
100% (HIGH) 3 minutes or until zucchini is
tender. Makes 2 servings.

# Colorful Squash Boats

Use half of acorn squash for this recipe and re-
mainder for another meal. It's easier to microwave
a whole squash than a half.

1 (l-lb.) acorn squash, pierced 4
   times
½ small green zucchini
1 small yellow zucchini or crookneck
   squash
2 tablespoons butter or margarine
⅛ teaspoon dried leaf basil
⅛ teaspoon dried leaf oregano
Fresh oregano, if desired

185

Place acorn squash in microwave oven. Microwave on 100% (HIGH) 7 to 8 minutes or until tender. Let stand 3 minutes. Cut in half lengthwise. Remove and discard seeds. Wrap and refrigerate one piece for another use. Cut remaining piece in half lengthwise. Set aside. Slice zucchini, and crookneck squash if using, in ¼-inch-thick rounds. Cut rounds in half to form semicircles. Alternate green and yellow squash semicircles in cavity of acorn squash. Set aside. In a custard cup, microwave butter or margarine on 100% (HIGH) 30 seconds. Remove from oven. Stir in basil and oregano. Brush mixture over squash. Wrap in plastic wrap. Microwave on 100% (HIGH) 3 to 4 minutes or until zucchini, and crookneck squash if using, are tender. Let stand, covered, 3 minutes. Garnish with oregano, if desired. Makes 2 servings.

# Swiss Broccoli

A delicious broccoli custard!

**1 (10-oz.) package frozen chopped broccoli**
**2 slices bacon, diced**

186

**1 tablespoon all-purpose flour**
**¼ cup finely chopped onion**
**½ cup sliced fresh mushrooms**
**¼ cup milk**
**2 eggs, beaten**
**½ cup (2-oz.) shredded Swiss cheese**

On a microwave-safe plate, microwave broccoli in package on 30% (MEDIUM-LOW) 10 minutes or until thawed. Remove broccoli from package; drain well. Set aside. Place bacon in a 2-cup microwave-safe casserole dish. Cover with wax paper. Microwave on 100% (HIGH) 2 to 2½ minutes or until crisp. Remove from oven. Stir in flour until dissolved, then onion and mushrooms. Microwave on 100% (HIGH) 1 minute. Set aside. In a small bowl, whisk milk and eggs. Mix in broccoli and cheese. Stir broccoli mixture into bacon mixture. Microwave on 70% (MEDIUM-HIGH) 3 minutes. Stir, bringing edges to center. Microwave on 70% (MEDIUM-HIGH) 2 to 4 minutes more or until center is set. Let stand 5 minutes. Makes 2 servings.

# Spinach Custard

Prepare Florentine Rice, page 115, with remaining spinach.

**1 (10-oz.) package frozen chopped spinach**
**½ cup half and half**
**2 eggs, beaten**
**Pinch ground nutmeg**
**¾ cup (3-oz.) shredded Swiss cheese**
**2 tablespoons all-purpose flour**

On a microwave-safe plate, microwave spinach in package on 30% (MEDIUM-LOW) 10 minutes or until thawed. Remove spinach from package; squeeze out as much liquid as possible. In a medium-size bowl, mix spinach, half and half, eggs and nutmeg. Dredge cheese in flour until all shreds are coated; stir into spinach mixture. Pour into 2 (10-oz.) microwave-safe soufflé dishes. Microwave on 70% (MEDIUM-HIGH) 2 minutes. Stir, bringing edges to center. Microwave on 70% (MEDIUM-HIGH) 2 to 2½ minutes more or until just set. Let stand 5 minutes. Makes 2 servings.

# Carrot Blossoms

Preparing vegetables in interesting ways can be fun and creative.

**1 thick chunky carrot, peeled**
**½ teaspoon chopped fresh dill**
**1 teaspoon water**
**Fresh dill sprig**

Cut off top of carrot. Cut 4 to 6 "V"-shaped wedges lengthwise running entire length of carrot. Slice crosswise in ¼-inch-thick slices. Place carrot, dill and water in a small microwave-safe serving dish. Cover tightly. Microwave on 100% (HIGH) 1½ minutes. Let stand, covered, 3 minutes. Garnish with dill sprig. Makes 1 serving.

**Variation**
*Zucchini Blossoms*: Substitute 1 medium-size zucchini for carrot.

# Vegetable Medley

Chill leftover vegetables and toss with a vinaigrette dressing for another meal.

**4 small white onions, peeled**
**1 medium-size carrot, peeled, thinly sliced**
**1 small zucchini, thinly sliced**
**1 tablespoon butter or margarine**
**1 tablespoon chopped fresh dill or 1 teaspoon dried dill weed**

Place onions, carrot, zucchini, butter or margarine and dill in a small microwave-safe casserole dish. Cover tightly. Microwave on 100% (HIGH) 3 minutes. Stir; re-cover. Microwave on 100% (HIGH) 1½ to 2 minutes more or until vegetables are tender-crisp. Let stand, covered, 3 minutes. Makes 2 servings.

# Swiss Mushrooms

Swiss cheese tops this unique vegetable dish.

**1 tablespoon butter or margarine**
**1 medium-size onion, thinly sliced**

**8 ounces small fresh mushrooms
1 tablespoon dry sherry
Pinch ground nutmeg
½ cup (2-oz.) shredded Swiss cheese**

In a small microwave-safe casserole dish, place butter or margarine and onion. Cover tightly. Microwave on 100% (HIGH) 2 minutes. Remove from oven. Stir in mushrooms, sherry and nutmeg; re-cover. Microwave on 100% (HIGH) 3 to 3½ minutes or until mushrooms are tender-crisp. Remove from oven. Sprinkle with cheese. Microwave on 100% (HIGH) 1 minute or until cheese melts. Makes 2 servings.

# *Marinated Mushrooms*

Serve as hors d'oeuvres, an appetizer, a salad or a side dish.

**2 tablespoons dry white wine
1 tablespoon olive oil
1 tablespoon lemon juice
1 small garlic clove, crushed
¼ teaspoon dried leaf basil
8 ounces medium-size fresh
   mushrooms
Lettuce leaves**

In a microwave-safe bowl, combine wine, olive oil, lemon juice, garlic, basil and mushrooms. Cover tightly. Microwave on 100% (HIGH) 3 to 4 minutes or until mushrooms are tender-crisp. Refrigerate at least 2 hours or until well-chilled and flavors are blended. Drain; serve on lettuce leaves. Makes 2 servings.

# Lemon Mint Peas

Cucumber shells containing lemon and mint flavored peas are assembled before microwaving.

**1 (10-oz.) cucumber, ends trimmed**
**2 fresh mint leaves**
**¾ cup frozen green peas**
**⅛ teaspoon grated lemon peel**
**1 teaspoon butter or margarine**
**2 fresh mint sprigs**

Using a zester, cut stripes down sides of cucumber. Cut in half crosswise. Using a small knife, trim around inside edge leaving a ⅛-inch rim. Using a small spoon, scoop out insides leaving a ½-inch thick bottom. Place a mint leaf in bottom of each cucumber cavity; fill with peas. Sprinkle with lemon peel.

Dot with butter or margarine. Place in a microwave-safe dish. Cover tightly. Micro-wave on 100% (HIGH) 1½ to 2 minutes or until peas are heated through. Garnish with mint sprigs. Makes 2 servings.

# SAUCES, GARNISHES & CONDIMENTS

The final appearance of microwaved foods often vary from those cooked conventionally. Microwaved vegetables are even more vibrant so they need little additional garnishing; some could even be considered a garnish themselves. Seafood, such as pink salmon or white halibut, keeps its lovely fresh color. A simple sauce or chopped fresh herbs sprinkled over the top is all that's needed. Meats and breads are two categories that usually need garnishing to make them more appealing. Garnishing can mean decorating the plate to add color or adding a sauce, a browning agent or a topping to make a pale food appear more appealing.

Garnishing a dish to make it look its best is always important whether you're serving one, two or 100 people. The eye plays a strong part in how we anticipate the flavor of food. Adding a sprig of fresh herb, cutting fresh vegetables in a decorative way or just using a colorful place setting can make any meal or snack special. And when you're serving food for one or two people, garnishing only takes a small amount of time and creativity. Carrot sticks spark up a plate; they're edible as well as beautiful. Cut a cherry tomato through the center two or three times, spread open to form a flower and place on a small lettuce leaf. If the amount of food is small and the plate large, thinly cut the stem of a green onion. It will gracefully curl and can be laid along the edge of a plate to fill it visually.

# Salsa Frita

Salsa is great for topping tacos or using as a dip for tortilla chips.

 1 tablespoon oil
 ¼ small onion, chopped
 1 garlic clove, chopped
 1 green bell pepper, seeded,
   chopped
 1 (8-oz.) can tomato sauce
 1 tablespoon finely chopped fresh
   cilantro (Chinese parsley or
   coriander)
 Salt
 Pepper

In a 2-cup glass measure, microwave oil, onion, garlic and bell pepper on 100% (HIGH) 1½ to 2 minutes or until onion is tender. Remove from oven. Stir in tomato sauce. Microwave on 100% (HIGH) 3 minutes. Stir in cilantro. Season to taste with salt and pepper. Cool, cover and refrigerate. Makes about 1¼ cups.

# Parmesan-Shrimp Sauce

Spinach pasta is my favorite with this sauce. Allow 2 ounces of uncooked pasta per serving.

**1 tablespoon butter or margarine**
**1 small garlic clove, minced**
**¼ medium-size onion, finely**
**    chopped**
**¼ green bell pepper, finely chopped**
**4 medium-size fresh mushrooms,**
**    thinly sliced**
**1 small tomato, seeded, finely**
**    chopped**
**4 ounces shrimp, peeled, deveined**
**½ cup dairy sour cream**
**¼ cup (¾-oz.) grated Parmesan**
**    cheese**

In a medium-size microwave-safe bowl, microwave butter or margarine and garlic on 100% (HIGH) 1 minute. Remove from oven. Stir in onion, bell pepper, mushrooms, tomato and shrimp. Cover tightly. Microwave on 100% (HIGH) 2 to 3 minutes or until vegetables are tender-crisp and shrimp are pink. Stir in sour cream and 2 tablespoons of cheese. If needed, microwave on 70% (MEDIUM-HIGH) 1½ minutes to reheat, stirring after 1 minute. Sprinkle with remaining cheese. Makes 2 servings.

# Tarragon-Mustard Sauce

A calorie-light seafood topping. Serve hot over poached fish fillets.

**1 tablespoon butter or margarine**
**1 tablespoon all-purpose flour**
**1½ teaspoons prepared mustard**
**¼ teaspoon salt**
**⅛ teaspoon dried leaf tarragon**
**Pinch paprika**
**½ cup milk**
**Chopped green onion stem, if**
**    desired**

In a 1-cup glass measure, microwave butter or margarine on 100% (HIGH) 15 to 20 seconds or until melted. Remove from oven. Stir in flour, mustard, salt, tarragon and paprika. Gradually add milk, stirring until well blended. Microwave on 100% (HIGH) 2 to

2½ minutes or just until thickened, stirring every 30 seconds. Sprinkle with green onion stem, if desired. Makes about ½ cup.

# Quick Béarnaise Sauce

Béarnaise sauce adds an elegant touch to any cut of beef or poultry. This is a tasty version.

**1 (3-oz.) package cream cheese**
**2 egg yolks, beaten**
**1 teaspoon minced onion**
**2 tablespoons dry white wine**
**1 teaspoon dried leaf tarragon**
**Fresh savory, if desired**

In a 2-cup glass measure, microwave cream cheese on 100% (HIGH) 20 seconds or until softened. Remove from oven. Stir in egg yolks, onion, wine and tarragon. Microwave on 100% (HIGH) 45 seconds, stirring every 15 seconds. Garnish with savory, if desired. Makes about ⅔ cup.

# Cranberry Sauce

Great on ham or poultry.

**2 teaspoons butter or margarine**
**2 tablespoons brown sugar**
**1 (8-oz.) can whole-berry cranberry**
   **sauce**
**½ (8¼-oz.) can crushed pineapple,**
   **juice packed**

In a small microwave-safe bowl, place butter or margarine, brown sugar, cranberry sauce and pineapple with juice. Microwave on 100% (HIGH) 1 minute; stir. Microwave on 100% (HIGH) 1½ minutes more or until bubbly; stir. Makes about ¾ cup.

# Flavored Butters

*South-of-the-Border Butter*

**1 tablespoon butter or margarine**
**Pinch chili powder**
**Pinch ground cumin**

In a custard cup, microwave butter or margarine, chili powder and cumin on 100%

(HIGH) 15 to 20 seconds or until butter or margarine melts; stir. Makes 1 serving.

*Oriental Butter*

---

**1 tablespoon butter or margarine**
**¼ teaspoon finely chopped fresh**
**cilantro (Chinese parsley or**
**coriander)**
**Pinch ground ginger**

In a custard cup, microwave butter or margarine, cilantro and ginger on 100% (HIGH) 15 to 20 seconds or until butter or margarine melts; stir. Makes 1 serving.

*Horseradish-Mustard Butter*

---

**1 tablespoon butter or margarine**
**⅛ teaspoon prepared horseradish**
**⅛ teaspoon prepared mustard**

In a custard cup, microwave butter or margarine, horseradish and mustard on 100% (HIGH) 15 to 20 seconds or until butter or margarine melts; stir. Makes 1 serving.

# Parmesan Cheese Sauce

Top steaming hot broccoli or toss with cooked pasta.

**1 tablespoon butter or margarine**
**1 tablespoon all-purpose flour**
**½ cup half and half**
**1 tablespoon thinly sliced green**
**   onion stem**
**1 tablespoon grated Parmesan**
**   cheese**

In a 1-cup glass measure, microwave butter or margarine on 100% (HIGH) 15 to 20 seconds or until melted. Remove from oven. Stir in flour, then half and half. Microwave on 100% (HIGH) 3 minutes or until mixture comes to a boil, stirring every minute. Remove from oven. Stir in green onion and cheese. Microwave on 100% (HIGH) 1 minute; stir. Makes about ¾ cup.

# Sherry-Mushroom Sauce

Use a chicken bouillon cube if sauce is served with poultry.

- **1 teaspoon cornstarch**
- **½ cup cold water**
- **1 beef bouillon cube**
- **1 teaspoon dry sherry**
- **¼ teaspoon Worcestershire sauce**
- **2 tablespoons thinly sliced fresh mushrooms**

In a 1-cup glass measure, dissolve cornstarch in water. Add bouillon cube, sherry and Worcestershire sauce. Microwave on 100% (HIGH) 2 to 2½ minutes or until mixture comes to a boil, stirring once. Remove from oven. Stir until bouillon cube dissolves. Stir in mushrooms. Microwave on 100% (HIGH) 1 minute; stir. Makes about ⅔ cup.

# Mock Hollandaise Sauce

Great for a vegetable or egg topping.

**2 tablespoons dairy sour cream**
**2 tablespoons mayonnaise**
**¼ teaspoon Dijon-style mustard**
**½ teaspoon lemon juice**

In a small custard cup, combine sour cream, mayonnaise, mustard and lemon juice. Microwave on 50% (**MEDIUM**) 1 minute or until heated through; stir. Makes ¼ cup.

# Tropical Barbecue Sauce

Brush on spareribs.

**1 (8-oz.) can crushed pineapple,**
**juice packed**
**¾ cup chili sauce**
**¼ cup packed brown sugar**
**½ teaspoon prepared mustard**

In a 2-cup glass measure, combine pineapple with juice, chili sauce, brown sugar and mustard. Microwave on 100% (HIGH) 4 to 4½ minutes or until mixture comes to a boil; stir. Makes 1½ cups.

# Marinara Sauce (Spaghetti Sauce)

Serve warm with a basket of soft French bread for dipping

    **8 ounces spicy bulk Italian sausage, crumbled**
**½ medium-size onion, chopped**
**1 stalk celery, thinly sliced**
**2 tablespoons pine nuts, chopped**
**1 (6-oz.) can tomato paste**
**⅛ teaspoon dried leaf basil**
**⅛ teaspoon dried leaf oregano**
**⅛ teaspoon Worcestershire sauce**
**⅛ teaspoon salt**
**Pinch garlic powder**
**Pinch pepper**

In a 1-quart microwave-safe casserole dish, microwave sausage, onion, celery and nuts on 100% (HIGH) 2 minutes. Stir to break up sausage and mix ingredients. Microwave on 100% (HIGH) 2 minutes more or until sausage is no longer pink. Drain well. Stir in tomato paste, basil, oregano, Worcestershire sauce, salt, garlic powder and pepper. Microwave on 100% (HIGH) 4 minutes; stir. If sauce is too thick, stir in a small amount of water. Makes about 3 cups sauce.

# Mustard Sauce

Serve with ham or pork.

- **1 tablespoon butter**
- **1 tablespoon all-purpose flour**
- **2 tablespoons white wine vinegar**
- **2 tablespoons sugar**
- **2 tablespoons prepared mustard**
- **2 tablespoons beef broth**

In a 2-cup glass measure, microwave butter on 100% (HIGH) 15 to 20 seconds or until melted. Remove from oven. Stir in flour, vinegar, sugar, mustard and beef broth. Microwave on 100% (HIGH) 1½ minutes or until mixture comes to a boil; stir. Makes ½ cup.

# Sweet & Sour Sauce

A tasty dipping sauce for meat balls served as an appetizer or an entrée.

> 1 teaspoon cornstarch
> ¼ cup packed brown sugar
> 2 tablespoons white vinegar
> ¼ cup unsweetened pineapple juice

In a 1-cup glass measure, mix cornstarch and brown sugar. Stir in vinegar and pineapple juice. Microwave on 100% (HIGH) 2 minutes; stir. Microwave on 100% (HIGH) 1 minute more or until slightly thickened; stir. Makes ½ cup.

# Pizza Sauce

Spread on a sliced French roll and sprinkle with your favorite toppings.

> 2 tablespoons finely chopped onion
> 1 tablespoon finely chopped green
>   bell pepper
> 1 (6-oz.) can tomato paste
> ¼ cup water
> ½ teaspoon sugar

¼ **teaspoon dried leaf oregano**
⅛ **teaspoon dried leaf thyme**
⅛ **teaspoon garlic salt**

In a small microwave-safe bowl, combine onion, bell pepper, tomato paste, water, sugar, oregano, thyme and garlic salt. Microwave on 100% (HIGH) 3 minutes, stirring once. Makes about ¾ cup.

# *Butter-Caper Sauce*

Serve over fish or vegetables.

**2 tablespoons butter or margarine**
⅛ **teaspoon dried leaf tarragon**
**2 capers, finely minced**

In a custard cup, microwave butter or margarine, tarragon and capers on 100% (HIGH) 20 to 30 seconds or until butter or margarine melts; stir. Makes 1 serving.

# Minted Vinegar Sauce

Great for lamb chops or shish kabobs.

- **1 tablespoon minced green onion**
- **½ cup white wine vinegar or rice vinegar**
- **2 tablespoons chopped fresh mint or 1 tablespoon dried leaf mint**
- **1 teaspoon sugar**

In a 1-cup glass measure, microwave green onion and vinegar on 100% (HIGH) 2 minutes. Stir in mint and sugar. Cool to room temperature; strain. Makes ½ cup.

# Sherry Glaze

Delicious on lamb or pork chops.

- **2 tablespoons brown sugar**
- **½ teaspoon cornstarch**
- **2 tablespoons dry sherry**
- **2 tablespoons orange juice**

In a 1-cup glass measure, combine brown sugar and cornstarch. Stir in sherry and orange juice. Microwave on 100% (HIGH) 1½ minutes. Makes ⅓ cup.

# *Hot Spicy Cranberry Glaze*

Spread on a slice of cooked turkey breast and heat for a real treat!

**1 (8-oz.) can whole-berry cranberry sauce**
**1 tablespoon apple juice or dry white wine**
**¼ teaspoon ground cinnamon**
**⅛ teaspoon ground nutmeg**

In a 1-cup glass measure, combine cranberry sauce, apple juice or wine, cinnamon and nutmeg. Microwave on 100% (HIGH) 2 to 3 minutes or until heated through; stir. Makes ½ cup.

# Sautéed Apple Slices

Serve with pork or turkey.

  **2 tablespoons butter**
  **1 teaspoon sugar**
  **Dash ground cinnamon**
  **Dash ground nutmeg**
  **1 cooking apple, cored, cut in ¼-
    inch-thick rings**

In a 9-inch microwave-safe pie plate, microwave butter, sugar, cinnamon and nutmeg on 100% (HIGH) 30 seconds. Remove from oven; stir. Add apples. Turn to coat both sides with butter mixture. Cover tightly. Microwave on 100% (HIGH) 2 minutes. Let stand, covered, 5 minutes. Makes 2 servings.

# Ginger-Peach Chutney

A sweet-savory accompaniment that goes well with beef, pork, lamb or poultry.

  **1 (8-oz.) can sliced peaches**
  **¼ cup raisins**
  **½ apple, cored, peeled, diced**

**1 teaspoon finely chopped
crystallized ginger
½ teaspoon cornstarch**

Drain peaches; reserve ¼ cup juice. Dice peaches. In a 2-cup glass measure, combine peaches, raisins, apple and ginger. Cover tightly. Microwave on 100% (HIGH) 4 minutes, stirring once. Remove from oven. In a 1-cup measure, dissolve cornstarch in reserved peach juice. Stir into peach mixture; re-cover. Microwave on 100% (HIGH) 2 minutes, stirring once. Cool to room temperature. Makes about 1 cup.

# Spiced Cranberry Relish

Fresh cranberries can be frozen up to one year.

**1 cup fresh or frozen cranberries
½ cup sugar
1 whole clove
1 (2-inch) piece cinnamon stick
1 teaspoon grated orange peel**

In a microwave-safe casserole dish, combine cranberries, sugar, clove, cinnamon stick and orange peel. Cover with wax paper. Microwave on 100% (HIGH) 3 minutes. Stir; re-cover. Microwave on 100% (HIGH) 1 to 2 minutes more or until mixture boils and berries start to pop open. Remove and discard clove and cinnamon stick. Makes about ¾ cup.

# Lemon Sauce

A perfect topping for gingerbread or persimmon pudding.

2½ tablespoons sugar
1 teaspoon cornstarch
⅓ cup water
1 teaspoon butter or margarine
1 teaspoon grated lemon peel
2 teaspoons fresh lemon juice

In a small microwave-safe bowl, combine sugar, cornstarch, water, butter or margarine, lemon peel and juice. Microwave on 100% (HIGH) 1 minute; stir. Microwave on 100% (HIGH) 1 to 1½ minutes more or until mixture comes to a boil and starts to thicken; stir. Makes ½ cup.

# Banana-Rum Ice Cream Topping

Pour over two scoops of vanilla ice cream for a delicious treat!

**2 tablespoons butter or margarine**
**2 tablespoons packed brown sugar**
**1 teaspoon grated orange peel**
**Juice ½ orange**
**2 tablespoons dark rum**
**1 small banana, sliced crosswise**

In a 2-cup microwave-safe casserole dish, microwave butter or margarine on 100% (HIGH) 20 to 30 seconds or until melted. Remove from oven. Stir in brown sugar, orange peel and juice and rum, then banana. Microwave on 100% (HIGH) 1 to 1½ minutes or until hot and bubbling around edges; stir. Makes 1 serving.

# Rum Custard Sauce

Serve over All-In-One-Pan Brownies, page 301.

**2 tablespoons sugar**
**2 teaspoons cornstarch**

217

½ cup milk
1 egg yolk, well beaten
1½ teaspoons butter
1 teaspoon rum
⅛ teaspoon vanilla extract

In a 2-cup glass measure, combine sugar and cornstarch. Add milk. Stir until cornstarch dissolves. Microwave on 70% (MEDIUM-HIGH) 2 minutes. Remove from oven. Stir until smooth. Beat small amount of hot liquid into egg yolk. Stir egg yolk into hot liquid. Microwave on 70% (MEDIUM-HIGH) 2 to 3 minutes or until mixture just starts to boil and thicken, stirring several times. Stir in butter, rum and vanilla. Makes ½ cup.

# *Caramel-Fudge Sauce*

Serve hot or cold over ice cream.

1 tablespoon butter
½ cup sugar
½ cup light corn syrup
¼ cup semi-sweet chocolate pieces
¼ cup milk

In a 2-cup glass measure, microwave butter on 100% (HIGH) 5 seconds or until softened.

Remove from oven. Stir in sugar and corn syrup. Microwave on 100% (HIGH) 4 to 5 minutes or until sugar dissolves, stirring once. Let stand 4 minutes. Stir in chocolate pieces until melted. Blend in milk. Makes 1 cup.

---

*Chef's Tip*
Lemons and oranges will be easier to squeeze and give more juice if microwaved on 100% (HIGH) 30 seconds or until warm.

# BREADS, GRAINS & PASTA

If up to now you have considered using your microwave oven only for microwaving vegetables and meats, defrosting and reheating, you are about to discover a new area—"baking." Successful "baking" can be done in a microwave oven. The standards are a little different than conventional ones, but the results can be very good. There are three basic differences to keep in mind because foods cook so quickly in a microwave oven. First: the texture will be fine grained, light and tender. Because it is very easy to overcook in a microwave oven, creating a chewy texture, always use the minimum time suggested. Second: foods "baked" in the microwave oven will differ in appearance because they will not brown. Where necessary, the recipes in this chapter use chocolate, molasses or other dark-color ingredients or add a topping such as streusel or icing to give food the expected look. Third: because microwave cooking creates moist heat, not a dry heat, a crispy crust will not form. Foods such as cream puffs or popovers will not work since they depend on a dry crust to give them shape and texture. Microwave cooking doesn't change the taste of foods.

Quick breads, muffins and cupcakes work very well in a microwave oven. Leavening agents work quickly, as soon as microwave energy creates heat in the food. Yeast breads are not good candidates for microwaving because of the long time needed for yeast to work and the dry heat needed to form an outer crust to support the bread. A microwave oven is a good place to proof yeast breads though. Fill a two-cup measure with water; place in the back of the microwave oven. Microwave on 100% (HIGH) five to six minutes or until water comes to a boil and creates steam. Turn the microwave oven off and place your rising bread dough inside and close the door. The steamy warmth of the oven is a perfect place for yeast to rise. Some manufacturer's instruction books say yeast bread can be microwaved on the lowest setting, but it requires close watching and results are not always perfect.

Round is the best shape for even cooking and the donut shape is even better. Square pans can be used with some shielding of the corners, but corners tend to cook quicker making them overcooked by the time the center is done. Greasing a microwave dish helps prevent sticking—but do not grease and flour any dish to be used in the microwave oven as a heavy layer is formed when microwaving. For easy removal of cakes or breads, I suggest lining the bottom of the dish with wax paper or coating with a cooking spray. For cupcakes or muffins, use paper baking cups to help keep their shape. Microwaves travel right through paper. Remove cupcakes and muffins as soon as they are done. Moisture gathers inside the cup and makes them soggy.

# Cinnamon-Raisin Muffins

Melt-in-your-mouth muffins!

**¼ cup quick-cooking rolled oats**
**¾ cup all-purpose flour**
**½ teaspoon baking powder**
**¼ teaspoon baking soda**
**⅛ teaspoon ground cinnamon**
**¼ cup packed brown sugar**
**½ cup buttermilk**
**1 egg, beaten**
**2 tablespoons vegetable oil**
**¼ cup raisins**
**1 tablespoon butter or margarine**
**1 tablespoon sugar**
**Pinch ground cinnamon**

Line 6 cups of a microwave-safe muffin ring or 6 custard cups with paper baking cups. In a medium-size bowl, combine oats, flour, baking powder, baking soda, ⅛ teaspoon cinnamon, and brown sugar. Set aside. In a 2-cup glass measure, combine buttermilk, egg, oil and raisins. Pour buttermilk mixture into dry mixture; mix until ingredients are just combined. Spoon batter in prepared cups filling half full. If using custard cups, arrange in a circle in microwave oven. Microwave on 100% (HIGH) 2 to 3 minutes or until muffins spring back when lightly touched. Remove muffins from cups to a wire rack. In a custard cup, microwave butter or margarine on 100% (HIGH) 15 to 20 seconds or until melted. Brush over tops of muffins. In a custard cup, combine sugar and pinch cinnamon. Sprinkle on muffins. Makes 6 muffins.

# Bran Muffins

Batter can be refrigerated up to two weeks. Microwave one or two muffins for breakfast each day.

**1¼ cup bran flakes**
**1 cup all-purpose flour**
**2 teaspoons baking powder**
**¼ teaspoon salt**
**1 egg, beaten**
**⅓ cup dark molasses**
**1 cup milk**
**¼ cup vegetable oil**
**2 teaspoons grated orange peel**
**½ cup raisins**

Line needed cups of a microwave-safe muffin ring or custard cups with paper baking cups. In a medium-size bowl, combine bran flakes, flour, baking powder and salt. Set aside. In a small bowl, combine egg, molasses, milk and vegetable oil. Stir egg mixture into flour mixture until ingredients are just combined. Mix in orange peel and raisins. Spoon batter into prepared cups filling half full. Microwave 1 muffin on 100% (HIGH) 30 seconds, 2 muffins on 100% (HIGH) 1 minute. Muffins should spring back when lightly touched. Remove muffins from cups to a wire rack to cool. Refrigerate remaining batter up to 2 weeks. Makes 14 muffins.

# French Onion-Cheese Muffins

A can of French fried onions will keep crisp if resealed tightly.

⅓ cup canned French fried onions, coarsely chopped
¾ cup buttermilk baking mix
¼ teaspoon onion salt
¼ cup (1-oz.) shredded Cheddar cheese

**1 egg, beaten**
**⅓ cup milk**
**2 tablespoons chopped green onion**
  **stems**

Line 6 cups of a microwave-safe muffin ring or 6 custard cups with paper baking cups. Reserve 3 tablespoons onions. In a small bowl, mix remaining onions, baking mix, onion salt, cheese, egg, milk and 1 tablespoon of green onion stems. Beat by hand 30 seconds. Spoon batter into prepared cups filling half full. Sprinkle with reserved onions, then remaining green onion stems. If using custard cups, arrange in a circle in microwave oven. Microwave on 100% (HIGH) 1½ to 2 minutes or until muffins spring back when lightly touched. Remove muffins from cups to a wire rack to cool. Makes 6 muffins.

---

*Chef's Tip*
To reheat bagels, rolls or quick breads, place a paper towel in microwave oven. Place bread on paper towel to absorb moisture. Microwave on 100% (HIGH) 6 to 7 seconds per roll. Microwaving a longer time results in cooking, not reheating.

# Muffins Primavera

Muffins with garden color and flavor.

1 tablespoon shredded carrot
1 tablespoon shredded zucchini
1 tablespoon chopped green onion
1 cup buttermilk baking mix
⅓ cup milk
1 egg, beaten
1 tablespoon shredded Cheddar
   cheese

Line 6 cups of a microwave-safe muffin ring or 6 custard cups with paper baking cups. In a small bowl, toss carrot, zucchini, green onion and baking mix. In a 1-cup glass measure, whisk milk, egg and cheese. Mix into dry ingredients until all ingredients are just combined. Spoon batter into prepared cups filling half full. If using custard cups, arrange in a circle in microwave oven. Microwave on 100% (HIGH) 4 to 6 minutes or until muffins spring back when lightly touched. Remove muffins from cups to a wire rack to cool. Makes 6 muffins.

# Corn Muffins

Corn muffins go great with just about anything.

**½ cup yellow cornmeal**
**½ cup all-purpose flour**
**1 tablespoon sugar**
**½ teaspoon baking powder**
**¼ teaspoon baking soda**
**¼ teaspoon salt**
**½ cup buttermilk**
**1 egg, beaten**

Line 6 cups of a microwave-safe muffin ring or 6 custard cups with paper baking cups. In a medium-size bowl, mix cornmeal, flour, sugar, baking powder, baking soda, salt, butter-milk and egg until just combined. Spoon batter into cups, filling half full. If using custard cups, arrange in a circle in microwave oven. Microwave on 100% (HIGH) 2 to 2½ minutes or until muffins spring back when lightly touched. Remove muffins from cups to a wire rack to cool. Makes 6 muffins.

To toast nuts, place ½ cup nuts in a pie plate. Microwave on 100% (HIGH) 2 minutes or until very hot, stirring frequently.

# Savory Apricot-Raisin Pilaf

Pilaf is Middle Eastern in origin. This recipe is an Americanized version.

**1 cup beef broth or chicken broth**
**1 tablespoon butter or margarine**
**1 cup quick-cooking rice**
**1 tablespoon diced dried apricots**
**1 tablespoon raisins**

In a 2-cup glass measure, microwave broth and butter or margarine on 100% (HIGH) 3 minutes or until mixture comes to a boil. Stir in rice, apricots and raisins. Cover tightly. Let stand 5 minutes or until rice has absorbed all liquid; stir. Makes 2 servings.

# Florentine Rice

Prepare Spinach Custard, page 94, with remaining spinach.

1 (10-oz.) package frozen chopped
   spinach
1 tablespoon pine nuts
1 cup cooked rice
1 egg, lightly beaten
½ cup creamed cottage cheese
1 tablespoon grated Parmesan
   cheese

On a microwave-safe plate, microwave spinach in package on 100% (HIGH) 2 to 3 minutes. Remove from package. Break apart; drain. Reserve ½ of spinach for another use. Place nuts on a microwave-safe plate in a single layer. Microwave on 100% (HIGH) 30 seconds. In a small bowl, combine spinach, nuts, rice, egg, cottage cheese and Parmesan cheese. Pour into a small round microwave-safe casserole dish. Microwave on 70% (MEDIUM-HIGH) 4 to 5 minutes or until mixture begins to set. Makes 2 servings.

# Quick Microwave Rice

Rice before you know it!

**½ cup water
1 teaspoon butter or margarine
Pinch salt
½ cup quick-cooking rice**

In a 2-cup glass measure, place water, butter or margarine and salt. Cover tightly. Microwave on 100% (HIGH) 2 minutes or until boiling. Stir in rice; re-cover. Let stand 5 minutes. Makes 1 serving.

# Spaghetti Tostada

Spaghetti can be cooked conventionally or microwaved; either way takes about the same amount of time.

**1 medium-size zucchini, cut
crosswise in ¼-inch slices
1 cup cooked spaghetti, drained
½ cup prepared spaghetti sauce or
Marinara Sauce, page 208
2 tablespoons shredded zucchini
2 tablespoons shredded carrot**

1 tablespoon chopped green onion
2 tablespoons shredded Monterey
Jack cheese

On a microwave-safe serving plate, arrange
zucchini slices overlapping in a circle. Spoon
spaghetti into center of plate; top with sauce.
Cover tightly. Microwave on 100% (HIGH)
3 minutes or until zucchini is tender-crisp
and spaghetti and sauce are heated through.
Sprinkle with shredded zucchini, carrot
and green onion, then cheese. Makes 1 serving.

# Pasta-Tuna Primavera

Fresh colored vegetables and tuna combine with
pasta in a sour cream sauce.

1 tablespoon olive oil
1 small garlic clove, minced
¼ small onion, sliced
½ cup broccoli flowerets
¼ cup sliced fresh mushrooms
½ small tomato, cut in thin wedges
½ small zucchini, thinly sliced

¼ teaspoon dried leaf oregano
1 (3¼-oz.) can solid white tuna,
  drained, flaked
½ cup dairy sour cream
2 cups hot cooked spaghetti, drained

In a small microwave-safe casserole dish, combine olive oil, garlic and onion. Cover tightly. Microwave on 100% (HIGH) 1 minute. Remove from oven. Stir in broccoli, mushrooms, tomato, zucchini, oregano and tuna; re-cover. Microwave on 100% (HIGH) 2½ to 3 minutes or until vegetables are tender. Stir in sour cream. Spoon spaghetti on 2 serving plates. Top with vegetable sauce. Makes 2 servings.

# French Bread & Flavored Spreads

*Parmesan Bread*

1 French roll, sliced lengthwise
Mayonnaise
Grated Parmesan cheese
Paprika

Lightly spread both halves of roll with mayonnaise. Sprinkle with cheese and paprika. Microwave on 100% (HIGH) 20 to 30 seconds or until warm.

*Dilly Bread*

---

**Thick slice of French bread or roll, cut in half lengthwise**
**Butter or margarine**
**Paprika**
**Fresh chopped dill**

Lightly spread bread with butter or margarine. Sprinkle lightly with paprika and dill. Microwave on 100% (HIGH) 20 to 30 seconds or until warm.

*Garlic Bread*

---

**Thick slice of French bread or roll cut in half lengthwise**
**Mayonnaise**
**Garlic salt**
**Paprika**

Lightly spread bread with mayonnaise. Sprinkle with garlic salt and paprika. Microwave on 100% (HIGH) 20 to 30 seconds or until warm.

# Savory Parmesan Ring

Herb-topped rolls easily pull apart.

**1 tablespoon butter or margarine**
**1 teaspoon water**
**3 tablespoons grated Parmesan cheese**
**¼ teaspoon paprika**
**½ teaspoon dried leaf basil**
**1 (4½-oz.) package refrigerated roll dough (6 rolls), separated**

In a 2-cup microwave-safe bowl, microwave butter or margarine on 100% (HIGH) 15 to 20 seconds or until melted. Remove from oven. Stir in water, cheese, paprika and basil. Dredge each roll in cheese mixture. On a microwave-safe flat serving plate, arrange rolls in a circle with sides touching. Microwave on 100% (HIGH) 1 to 1½ minutes or until dough appears dry. Makes 6 rolls.

# Scones

Serve with whipped cream and strawberry jam.

1¼ cups all-purpose flour
1 teaspoon baking powder
2½ teaspoons sugar
1 tablespoon butter or margarine
3 tablespoons dried currants or
 raisins
3 tablespoons milk
¼ teaspoon vanilla extract
1 egg, beaten
⅛ teaspoon cinnamon

In a medium-size bowl, combine flour, baking powder and 2 teaspoons of sugar. Using a pastry blender or 2 knives, cut in butter or margarine until mixture resembles coarse crumbs. Mix in currants or raisins, milk, vanilla and egg. When dough is smooth, knead 4 to 5 times. Shape in a 5-inch circle. Place on a flat microwave-safe plate. Cut in 6 wedges. In a custard cup, combine remaining sugar and cinnamon. Sprinkle scones with sugar mixture. Microwave on 70% (MEDIUM-HIGH) 1 to 2 minutes or just until dry. Remove to a wire rack to cool. Makes 6 scones.

# Dutch Apple Pancake

Peaches are a wonderful substitute for apples.

**2 tablespoons butter or margarine**
**½ cup thinly sliced peeled apples**
**3 tablespoons sugar**
**¼ teaspoon grated lemon peel**
**Pinch ground nutmeg**
**⅓ cup buttermilk baking mix**
**⅛ teaspoon ground cinnamon**
**2 tablespoons water**
**⅛ teaspoon vanilla extract**

In a 2½ cup microwave-safe round casserole dish, place butter or margarine, apples, 2 tablespoons of sugar, lemon peel and nutmeg. Cover tightly. Microwave on 100% (HIGH) 1½ to 2 minutes or until butter or margarine melts. Stir; set aside. In a small bowl, combine remaining 1 tablespoon of sugar, baking mix, cinnamon, water and vanilla. Spoon over apple mixture. Microwave on 100% (HIGH) 1½ to 2 minutes or until set. Invert on a serving plate. Makes 2 servings.

To soften "too-dry" dried fruit, place ½ cup dried fruit in a microwave-safe glass dish. Sprinkle with ½ to 1 teaspoon water. Cover tightly. Microwave on 100% (HIGH) 15 to 30 seconds.

# Steamed Boston Brown Bread

To sour milk quickly, add 1 teaspoon lemon juice to ½ cup milk; let stand 5 minutes.

> **½ cup buttermilk or soured milk**
> **¼ cup dark molasses**
> **⅓ cup raisins**
> **½ cup all-purpose flour**
> **¼ cup cornmeal**
> **¼ teaspoon baking soda**
> **½ teaspoon salt**

Generously grease a 2-cup glass measure. In a small bowl, combine buttermilk, molasses and raisins. Stir in flour, cornmeal, baking soda and salt; mix well. Pour into prepared measure. Cover tightly. Microwave on 50% (MEDIUM) 4 minutes. Rotate container a half turn. Microwave on 50% (MEDIUM) 2 to 3 minutes more or until mixture is set. Let stand, covered, 5 minutes. Invert on a serving plate. Makes 2 servings.

# Sour Cream-Blueberry Bread

Serve for a special Sunday brunch.

⅓ **cup sugar**
**3 tablespoons butter or margarine**
**1 egg yolk**
½ **teaspoon vanilla extract**
¾ **cup all-purpose flour**
½ **teaspoon baking soda**
**Pinch salt**
½ **cup dairy sour cream**
½ **cup fresh or frozen blueberries**

Grease an 8″ × 4″ microwave-safe glass loaf pan. In a small bowl, cream sugar and butter or margarine until fluffy. Stir in egg yolk and vanilla. Add flour, baking soda, salt and sour cream; mix well. Stir in berries. Pour into prepared pan. Microwave on 50% (MEDIUM) 5 to 7 minutes or until top looks dry, rotating dish every 2 minutes. Let stand on a flat heatproof surface 5 minutes. Remove from pan to a wire rack. Makes 1 loaf.

*Chef's Tip*
To shell pecans or walnuts easily and with less breakage, place 2 cups nuts and 1 cup water in a microwave-safe glass dish. Cover tightly. Microwave on 100% (HIGH) 1 to 2 minutes.

# *Apple Pinwheel Coffeecake*

For a weekend treat, serve with Cinnamon Cocoa, page 36.

**1 tablespoon packed brown sugar**
**¼ medium-size apple, peeled, cored, cut in ¼-inch slices**
**1 tablespoon butter or margarine**
**1 egg yolk, lightly beaten**
**3 tablespoons milk**
**⅔ cup all-purpose flour**
**2 tablespoons sugar**
**½ teaspoon baking powder**
**1 tablespoon finely chopped walnuts**

Sprinkle brown sugar in a 10-ounce micro-wave-safe soufflé dish. Arrange apple slices slightly overlapping forming a circle on top of brown sugar. Dot with butter or margarine. In a small bowl, mix egg yolk, milk, flour, sugar, baking powder and walnuts. Spoon over apples. Microwave on 100% (HIGH) 1½ to 2 minutes or until batter is set but edges are still moist. Let stand 5 minutes. Makes 2 servings.

---

*Chef's Tip*

To soften 1 cup brown sugar, place sugar in a microwave-safe bowl. Cover tightly. Microwave on 100% (HIGH) 30 seconds or until softened. Check often.

---

# *BREAKFAST*

Breakfast is usually prepared in a hurry and, since a microwave oven cooks in a hurry, it's the perfect solution to this early meal. Heat water for your tea or instant coffee right in a mug, then microwave hot cereal in a serving bowl. Pop in a couple of bran muffins, microwave in less than one minute, and you've got breakfast covered. Quick, easy and with a minimum of dishes to wash.

On those days you want to spend more time and thought on preparation, try a Zucchini Frittata with bacon. Microwave bacon on paper towels to absorb fat and then discard the paper towels. The bacon stays flat, cleanup is extra easy and you'll quickly forget how grease spatters when bacon is cooked in a skillet. Even a poached egg can be microwaved. While the egg is microwaving, pop a slice of bread in the toaster and breakfast is served.

Brunch served with the Sunday paper is a lovely way to spend a leisurely morning. Try the Mexican Egg Rolls with a Baked Apple. A microwave oven can help with other breakfast tasks such as warming syrup for pancakes. Make a quick batch of Strawberry Preserves to serve with waffles or try the Quick Apple Butter on a bagel.

With a microwave oven to speed up breakfast preparation, there's no excuse to skip this important meal, even if you're late getting up.

# Mexican Egg Rolls

What a way to start your day!

**4 eggs**
**2 tablespoons water**
**1 teaspoon finely chopped fresh cilantro (Chinese parsley or coriander), if desired**
**2 tablespoons chopped green onion**
**2 (8-inch) flour tortillas**
**½ avocado, thinly sliced**
**¼ cup Salsa Frita, page 199, or taco sauce**
**⅓ cup (1½ oz.) shredded Cheddar cheese**
**Fresh cilantro sprigs, if desired**

In a microwave-safe bowl, whisk eggs, water, chopped cilantro and green onion. Microwave on 100% (HIGH) 2 minutes; stir. Microwave on 100% (HIGH) 1 to 2 minutes more or until eggs are set. Spoon egg mixture down center of tortillas. Top with avocado and Salsa Frita or taco sauce. Sprinkle with cheese. Fold sides of tortilla over filling to center. Fold bottom over filling and roll up, jelly roll style, enclosing filling completely.

Place, folded side down, on 2 microwave-safe plates. Microwave each egg roll on 100% (HIGH) 30 seconds. Garnish with cilantro, if desired. Makes 2 servings.

# Perfect Poached Egg

A fool-proof method for a poached egg every time!

**¼ cup water**
**¼ teaspoon vinegar**
**1 egg**

Combine water and vinegar in a custard cup. Break egg into cup. Prick yolk once with a fork. Cover with wax paper. Microwave on 100% (HIGH) 1 to 1½ minutes or until set. Using a spoon, remove egg from water, draining well. Makes 1 serving.

# Sunny Side Up

I always cook extra rice because it can be refrigerated up to 7 days.

**1 teaspoon chopped green onion**
**1 teaspoon chopped red bell pepper**
**1 teaspoon butter or margarine**

⅓ cup cooked rice
1 egg
1 tablespoon shredded Cheddar
   cheese

In a small microwave-safe casserole dish, microwave green onion, bell pepper and butter or margarine on 100% (HIGH) 1 minute. Stir in rice. Microwave on 100% (HIGH) 1 to 1½ minutes or until hot. Remove from oven. Using a spoon, make a hollow in center of rice. Break egg into hollow. Pierce yolk once with a fork. Cover tightly. Microwave on 100% (HIGH) 1 minute or until egg is set. Sprinkle with cheese. Makes 1 serving.

# Salmon Benedict

Eggs Benedict is said to be named after a Mrs. Benedict who requested the combination at Delmonico's Restaurant in New York in the late 1800's.

1 (7¾-oz.) can salmon, drained, skin
   and bones removed and discarded
2 English muffins, split, toasted,
   buttered
4 eggs

**1 recipe Mock Hollandaise Sauce,
    page 207
Paprika**

Using a fork, flake salmon. Spoon onto muffin halves. Break each egg into a custard cup. Pierce each yolk once with a fork. Cover tightly. Microwave on 70% (MEDIUM-HIGH) 2 to 3 minutes or until yolks are done as desired. Place one egg on each muffin. Prepare Mock Hollandaise Sauce as directed. Top egg with sauce. Sprinkle with paprika. Makes 2 servings.

# Red, White & Green Omelet

To reheat leftover omelet, cover tightly and microwave on 100% (HIGH) 15 to 30 seconds.

**2 slices bacon
1 cup frozen hash-brown potatoes
    broken in small chunks
1 tablespoon chopped onion
1 tablespoon chopped green bell
    pepper
1 tablespoon chopped red bell
    pepper**

**2 eggs**
**2 tablespoons milk**
**¼ cup (2-oz.) shredded Cheddar cheese**

Lay bacon strips flat in a 1-quart microwave-safe casserole dish. Cover with a paper towel. Microwave on 100% (HIGH) 1½ to 2 minutes or until bacon is crisp. Remove from oven; cool. Crumble bacon back into dish. Stir in potatoes, onion and green and red bell peppers. Microwave on 100% (HIGH) 3 minutes, stirring once. Remove from oven. Set aside. In a small bowl, whisk eggs and milk. Pour over potato mixture. Microwave on 70% (MEDIUM-HIGH) 3 to 4 minutes or until eggs are set, stirring after 2 minutes. Sprinkle with cheese. Let stand 3 minutes or until cheese melts. Makes 2 servings.

*Chef's Tip*
Microwave bacon on paper towels so no draining is necessary. For bacon bits, cut bacon in pieces before microwaving.

# Scrambled Eggs

Stir in shredded cheese for a treat.

**2 eggs**
**2 teaspoons water**
**Salt**
**Pepper**

Line a microwave-safe bowl with parchment paper. If needed, attach parchment paper to bottom of bowl with a piece of tape. In a small bowl, beat eggs and water. Pour into prepared dish. Microwave on 100% (HIGH) 1½ to 2 minutes or until almost set, stirring once. Eggs will be slightly moist. Let stand 3 minutes. Season to taste with salt and pepper. Makes 2 servings.

# Huevo Rancheros

An egg ranch-style, a popular Mexican dish.

**1 (6-inch) corn tortilla**
**⅓ cup refried beans**
**1 egg**
**2 tablespoons Salsa Frita, page 199, or taco sauce**

1 teaspoon chopped green onion
2 tablespoons shredded Cheddar
  cheese

Place tortilla on a microwave-safe serving plate. Spread beans on tortilla leaving a ½-inch rim around outer edge. Using a spoon, make a small hollow in center of beans. Break egg into hollow. Pierce yolk once with a fork. Microwave on 70% (MEDIUM-HIGH) 1½ to 2 minutes or until egg is set. Top with Salsa Frita or taco sauce and green onion. Sprinkle with cheese. Makes 1 serving.

# Baked Apple

For an attractive appearance and to help steam escape, cut a wide strip of peel from top of apple.

1 tablespoon raisins
1 tablespoon packed brown sugar
Pinch ground cinnamon
⅛ teaspoon grated lemon peel
1 medium-size baking apple, cored

In a custard cup, combine raisins, brown sugar, cinnamon and lemon peel. Pack center of apple with raisin mixture. Place apple in a microwave-safe bowl. Cover tightly. Microwave on 100% (HIGH) 2 to 2½ minutes or until apple is tender. Let stand, covered, 5 minutes. Makes 1 serving.

# Granola

Refrigerate tightly covered. You'll never buy packaged cereal again.

> 1 cup regular rolled oats
> ¼ cup wheat germ
> 1 tablespoon finely chopped almonds
> 1 tablespoon sunflower seeds
> 1 tablespoon sesame seeds
> 2 tablespoons shredded unsweetened coconut
> 2 tablespoons honey
> 1 tablespoon vegetable oil
> 3 pitted dates, finely chopped
> 2 tablespoons raisins

In a microwave-safe bowl, combine oats, wheat germ, almonds, sunflower seeds, sesame seeds and coconut. In a 1-cup glass measure, combine honey and oil. Microwave on 100% (HIGH) 15 seconds. Pour over oat mixture. Stir to coat all ingredients. Microwave on 100% (HIGH) 2 minutes; stir. Microwave on 100% (HIGH) 1½ to 2 minutes more or until toasted. Stir in dates and raisins. Cool to room temperature. Store in a jar with a tight-fitting lid. Makes 1¾ cups.

# Quick Apple Butter

An extra fast way to make apple butter.

**1 cup unsweetened applesauce**
**½ cup packed brown sugar**
**Pinch ground nutmeg**
**¼ teaspoon ground cinnamon**
**1 teaspoon lemon juice**

In a 4-cup glass measure, combine applesauce, brown sugar, nutmeg, cinnamon and lemon juice. Microwave on 100% (HIGH) 3 to 4 minutes or until mixture comes to a boil; stir. Microwave on 100% (HIGH) 2 minutes more. Pour into a sterilized 8-ounce jar. Cool, cover tightly and refrigerate. Makes about 1¼ cups.

# Strawberry Preserves

If using frozen strawberries packed in syrup, decrease sugar to 1 cup.

**1 pint fresh or 1 (16-oz.) package frozen strawberries, halved or sliced**
**1⅓ cups sugar**
**1 tablespoon powdered pectin or 2 tablespoons liquid pectin**
**1½ to 2 tablespoons lemon juice**

In a 2-quart microwave-safe casserole dish, combine strawberries, sugar, pectin and lemon juice. Microwave on 100% (HIGH) 7 to 8 minutes or until mixture boils, stirring several times. Microwave on 100% (HIGH) 1 minute more. Cool to room temperature, stirring occasionally. Mixture will be very thin and thicken as it cools. Pour into 2 sterilized 8-ounce jars. Cool, cover tightly and refrigerate. Makes 2 cups.

# Quick Buttersyrup

Great for pancakes or waffles.

**2 tablespoons butter or margarine
2 tablespoons maple-flavored syrup**

In a custard cup, microwave butter or margarine and syrup on 100% (HIGH) 30 to 45 seconds or until butter or margarine is completely melted; stir. Makes ¼ cup.

Try on Scones, page 240, Cinnamon-Raisin Muffins, page 227.

# Strawberry Pancake Syrup

If desired, unstrained strawberries may be used.

**1 (10-oz.) package frozen
   unsweetened strawberries
½ cup light corn syrup**

Line a strainer with cheesecloth or use a very fine gauge strainer. Set in a microwave-safe bowl. Remove metal top from strawberry package. Microwave on 50% (MEDIUM) 10 minutes. Pour berries and juice into strainer. Using back of a spoon, press all juice from berries. Discard pulp. Pour berry juice into a small bowl. Stir corn syrup into berry juice. Microwave on 100% (HIGH) 3 to 4 minutes or until mixture comes to a rolling boil. Using a metal spoon, skim foam from top. Pour into a sterilized 8-ounce jar. Cool, cover tightly and refrigerate. Makes about 1 cup.

**Variation**
Substitute frozen raspberries for strawberries.

# *Kiwifruit Breakfast Topping*

Serve warm on pancakes, waffles or French toast, or cool and use like jam on toast, muffins or bagels.

**1 kiwifruit, peeled, thinly sliced**
**¼ cup honey**
**1½ tablespoons orange juice**
**1 teaspoon butter or margarine**
**⅛ teaspoon grated orange peel**

Cut each kiwifruit slice in quarters. Set aside. In a 1-cup glass measure, microwave honey, orange juice, butter or margarine and orange peel on 100% (HIGH) 20 to 30 seconds or until mixture is boiling. Stir in kiwifruit. Makes ½ cup.

# Sweet Applesauce

A delicious treat for breakfast or anytime!

**2 medium-size apples, peeled, cored, chopped**
**2 tablespoons sugar**
**⅛ teaspoon ground cinnamon**

In a 1-quart microwave-safe casserole dish, combine apples, sugar and cinnamon. Cover tightly. Microwave on 100% (HIGH) 3 to 3½ minutes. Stir; recover. Let stand 10 minutes. Serve warm or chilled. Makes 2 servings.

# Ambrosia Topping

Serve over French toast, either homemade or from the frozen section in your supermarket. Both re-heat beautifully in a microwave oven.

½ (8-oz.) can crushed pineapple, juice packed
½ orange, cut in sections
2 tablespoons shredded unsweetened coconut
½ teaspoon cornstarch
Dash ground nutmeg

In a small microwave-safe bowl, combine pineapple with juice, orange, coconut, cornstarch and nutmeg. Microwave on 100% (HIGH) 3 to 4 minutes or until mixture is slightly thickened, stirring once. Makes ¾ cup.

---

*Chef's Tip*
To heat syrup, microwave ½ cup syrup in a 1-cup glass measure on 100% (HIGH) 45 seconds.

---

# *LIGHT MEALS*

Three square heavy meals a day are no longer the norm in our mobile society. Eating lighter seems to be an important and healthy concept. Perhaps you've had a large lunch and feel like a light dinner. Look through this chapter to find just what you want. A Shrimp-Stuffed Artichoke is a meal in itself. An artichoke is usually considered the vegetable part of a whole meal but, with this savory filling, it qualifies as a main dish.

Tacos for Two can serve one or two, or triple the recipe and have a party for six. The traditional meat, cheese and lettuce ingredients can be altered to fit your taste preferences. If you prefer only vegetables, use only vegetables. A microwave oven can cook several varieties quickly. Stuff vegetables into a taco shell and top with salsa. A microwave oven can quickly cook to your whims, so recipe changes are easy.

A light meal can be one item like Welsh Rabbit, which has several ingredients, or just

267

a simple toasted cheese sandwich. Depending on how hungry you are, add a salad, steam some vegetables or make Chocolate Mousse from the Dessert Chapter to finish off your meal.

# Picante-Stuffed Pepper

This recipe can easily be doubled. Microwave on 100% (HIGH) 2½ to 3 minutes or until heated.

1 large red, green or yellow bell pepper
6 ounces ground beef or ground turkey, crumbled
¼ cup finely chopped onion
¼ cup dry bread crumbs
⅛ teaspoon Worcestershire sauce
⅛ teaspoon garlic salt
Dash pepper
¼ cup Salsa Frita, page 199
¼ cup kidney beans, drained
1 teaspoon finely chopped fresh cilantro (Chinese parsley or coriander)
Fresh cilantro sprigs

Cut off top ⅓ of pepper. Remove and discard seeds. Set pepper aside. In a small microwave-safe bowl, combine beef or turkey, onion and bread crumbs. Microwave on 100% (HIGH) 2 minutes. Stir to break up beef or turkey in small chunks; drain, if necessary.

Stir in Worcestershire sauce, garlic salt, pepper, Salsa Frita, beans and chopped cilantro. Lightly pack beef or turkey mixture into pepper. Place pepper on a microwave-safe plate. Cover tightly. Microwave on 100% (HIGH) 1½ to 2 minutes or until heated through. Garnish with cilantro sprigs. Makes 1 serving.

# Eggplant Enchiladas

Use either canned enchilada sauce or reconstituted enchilada sauce mix.

**1 tablespoon butter or margarine**
**2 tablespoons chopped onion**
**1 cup peeled cubed eggplant**
**½ cup sliced zucchini**
**¼ cup chopped tomato**
**1 cup enchilada sauce**
**4 (8-inch) flour tortillas**
**½ cup (2-oz.) shredded Monterey**
  **Jack cheese**

In a small microwave-safe bowl, combine butter or margarine, onion, eggplant, zucchini and tomato. Cover tightly. Microwave on 100% (HIGH) 2 to 3 minutes or until vegetables are tender. Pour enchilada sauce into a shallow dish. Dip tortilla into sauce, coating both sides. Spread ¼ of eggplant mixture down center of tortilla to ¼-inch from edge. Fold sides of tortilla towards center, overlapping. Place, folded side down, in a microwave-safe dish. Repeat with remaining tortillas. Pour remaining sauce over enchiladas. Sprinkle with cheese. Cover tightly. Microwave on 100% (HIGH) 3 to 4 minutes or until cheese is melted. Makes 2 servings.

# Oriental Enchiladas

Tortillas with a "stir-fry" type filling.

- **1 tablespoon soy sauce**
- **1 teaspoon Dijon-style mustard**
- **1 teaspoon dry sherry**
- **⅛ teaspoon ground ginger**
- **1 (4-oz.) boneless skinned chicken breast half, cut in ½-inch pieces**
- **4 to 6 Chinese pea pods**
- **6 medium-size fresh mushrooms, sliced**
- **1 green onion, thinly sliced**
- **1 small tomato, seeded, thinly sliced**
- **1 teaspoon cornstarch**
- **¼ cup chicken broth**
- **4 (8-inch) flour tortillas**

In a medium-size microwave-safe bowl, combine soy sauce, mustard, sherry, ginger and chicken. Let stand 10 minutes. Microwave on 100% (HIGH) 2 minutes. Remove from oven. Stir in pea pods, mushrooms, green onion and tomato. In a 1-cup glass measure, dissolve cornstarch in chicken broth. Pour over chicken and vegetable mixture. Cover tightly. Microwave on 100% (HIGH) 1 to 2 minutes or until chicken turns from translucent to opaque and vegetables are tender. Spread ¼ of chicken mixture down center of each tortilla to ¼-inch from edge. Fold sides of tortillas towards center, overlapping. Place enchiladas, folded side down, on a microwave-safe serving plate. Microwave on 100% (HIGH) 1½ to 2 minutes or until heated through. Makes 2 servings.

# Welsh Rabbit

History has it that a Welsh nobleman ran out of game to serve his guests, so he served cheese and called it Welsh Rabbit.

**1 tablespoon butter or margarine**
**1 tablespoon all-purpose flour**
**½ cup beer, room temperature**

1 teaspoon Dijon-style mustard
¼ teaspoon Worcestershire sauce
1 cup (4-oz.) shredded sharp
   Cheddar cheese
2 English muffins, split, toasted
4 slices tomato, cut in halves

In a 2-cup glass measure, microwave butter or margarine on 100% (HIGH) 15 to 20 seconds or until melted. Remove from oven. Stir in flour. Whisk in beer, mustard and Worcestershire sauce. Microwave on 100% (HIGH) 2 minutes. Remove from oven. Stir in cheese until melted. Microwave on 50% (MEDIUM) 2 minutes. Place 2 muffin halves in each of 2 ramekins or on 2 microwave-safe serving plates. Spoon cheese sauce over muffins. Garnish with tomato slices. Makes 2 servings.

# Shrimp-Stuffed Artichoke

Crab can be substituted for the shrimp.

2 (8-oz.) artichokes
1 (7½-oz.) can bay shrimp, well
   drained

¼ **cup mayonnaise**

**1 teaspoon lemon juice**

½ **cup (2-oz.) shredded Cheddar cheese**

**2 tablespoons finely chopped green onion**

Slice off top 1-inch of artichokes so top is flat. Using scissors, snip off point from each leaf. Rinse under cool water. Drain, but do not shake off all water. Wrap individually in plastic wrap. Place in microwave oven upside down. Microwave on 100% (HIGH) 7 to 8 minutes or until heart is tender when pierced from bottom. Do not unwrap. Let stand 5 minutes. In a small bowl, combine shrimp, mayonnaise, lemon juice, cheese and green onion. Pull center leaves from artichoke. Using a spoon, scoop out choke. Fill center of each artichoke with shrimp mixture. Place in a medium-size microwave-safe dish. Cover tightly. Microwave on 100% (HIGH) 1½ to 2 minutes or until filling is heated through. Makes 2 servings.

# English Muffin Pizzas

Use any favorite toppings.

**1 English muffin, split, toasted**
**3 to 4 tablespoons Pizza Sauce, page 210**
**Assorted toppings: sliced pepperoni, crushed pineapple, chopped pine nuts, sliced mushrooms, sliced olives, sliced zucchini**
**2 tablespoons shredded provolone, Cheddar or Monterey Jack cheese**

Place a paper towel in bottom of microwave oven. Spread muffin halves with sauce. Sprinkle with toppings, then cheese. Place muffin halves on paper towel. Microwave on 70% (MEDIUM-HIGH) 1 to 1½ minutes or until cheese begins to melt. Makes 1 serving.

# Zucchini Frittata

A frittata is similar to a crustless quiche.

**2 eggs**
**1 medium-size zucchini, shredded**
**¼ cup finely chopped onion**

**2 tablespoons finely chopped red
  bell pepper**
**4 fresh mushrooms, thinly sliced**
**2 teaspoons dry white wine**
**⅛ teaspoon salt**
**Dash pepper**
**½ cup (2-oz.) shredded Cheddar
  cheese**

In a medium-size bowl, whisk eggs. Stir in zucchini, onion, bell pepper, mushrooms, wine, salt and pepper. Pour into a 6-inch oval microwave-safe casserole dish. Microwave on 70% (MEDIUM-HIGH) 2 minutes. Stir, bringing outside to center. Microwave on 70% (MEDIUM-HIGH) 2 minutes more or until eggs are just set. Sprinkle with cheese. Makes 2 servings.

# Quesadilla

Use jalapeño chilies if you like food hot; use Anaheim chilies for a milder flavor.

**1 (10-inch) flour tortilla**
**¼ cup (1-oz.) shredded Cheddar
  cheese**
**1 tablespoon chopped green chilies**

2 teaspoons chopped green onion
2 tablespoons Salsa Frita, page 199,
  if desired
¼ cup dairy sour cream
Guacamole, if desired

Sprinkle ½ of tortilla with cheese, green chilies, green onion and Salsa Frita, if desired. Fold in half. On a microwave-safe serving plate, microwave on 100% (HIGH) 1 minute or until cheese melts. Top with sour cream and guacamole, if desired. Makes 1 quesadilla.

# *Raclette*

Melted cheese is eaten with potatoes, gherkins and French bread.

3 to 4 small new potatoes, pierced
4 ounces Swiss cheese or raclette,
  cut in ½-inch-thick slices
4 to 5 gherkins

Place potatoes in microwave oven. Microwave on 100% (HIGH) 3 minutes. Turn potatoes over. Microwave on 100% (HIGH) 1 to 3 minutes more or until potatoes give slightly when squeezed. Wrap in foil. Set aside. Place cheese on a microwave-safe serving plate. Microwave on 70% (MEDIUM-HIGH) 1 to 3 minutes or just until cheese softens. Set aside. Thinly slice gherkins lengthwise almost to end 4 to 5 times. Fan out on serving plate with cheese. Unwrap and place potatoes on plate. If needed, microwave on 70% (MEDIUM-HIGH) 15 to 30 seconds to reheat. Makes 2 servings.

# Tortilla Quiche

Serve with fruit salad and a glass of wine for a great light dinner.

**1 (10-oz.) package frozen spinach**
**1 (8-inch) flour tortilla**
**2 eggs, beaten**
**2 tablespoons milk**
**¼ cup (1-oz.) shredded Swiss cheese**
**Pinch ground nutmeg**

Place spinach in package on a microwave-safe plate. Microwave on 100% (HIGH) 4 minutes. Remove spinach from package. Drain well. Reserve ½ of spinach for another use. Place a paper towel in bottom of microwave oven. Place tortilla on paper towel. Microwave on 100% (HIGH) 5 to 10 seconds or until softened. Shape tortilla to fit in a 1½ to 2-cup microwave-safe ramekin or soufflé dish. In a small bowl, whisk spinach, eggs, milk, cheese and nutmeg. Pour mixture in center of tortilla. Microwave on 70% (MEDIUM-HIGH) 2 to 3 minutes or until edges of quiche are set. Let stand 5 minutes. Makes 1 serving.

---

*Chef's Tip*
Reheating can be done on 100% (HIGH), but food probably will need to be stirred or rotated sometime during the cooking process.

---

# *Florentine Eggs*

Individual casseroles are an elegant way to serve this dish.

**1 (10-oz.) package frozen chopped spinach**
**¼ cup (1-oz.) shredded Swiss cheese**
**2 teaspoons dry onion soup mix**
**2 tablespoons water**
**2 thin slices ham**

**1 tomato, cut in 6 wedges**
**2 eggs**

Place spinach in package on a microwave-safe plate. Microwave on 100% (HIGH) 4 minutes. Remove spinach from package. Drain well. In a small bowl, mix spinach, cheese, soup mix and water. Line 2 (10-oz.) microwave-safe casserole dishes with ham. Fill with spinach mixture. Arrange 3 tomato wedges to form a triangle in center of spinach. Break an egg into each triangle. Pierce yolks once with a fork. Microwave on 70% (MEDIUM-HIGH) 2 to 3 minutes or until eggs are almost set. Makes 2 servings.

# *Frankfurter Bean Pot*

Perfect for a cold winter day.

**2 tablespoons chopped onion**
**1 can (8-oz.) pork and beans**
**1 tablespoon ketchup**
**2 teaspoons packed brown sugar**
**½ teaspoon prepared mustard**
**1 to 2 frankfurters, each cut in 5 pieces**

Place onion in a small microwave-safe casserole dish. Cover tightly. Microwave on 100% (HIGH) 1 to 1½ minutes or until tender. Remove from oven. Stir in beans, ketchup, brown sugar, mustard and frankfurters; re-cover. Microwave on 100% (HIGH) 2 minutes. Remove from oven. Stir, pushing pieces of frankfurter beneath beans; re-cover. Microwave on 100% (HIGH) 1 to 2 minutes more or until heated through. Makes 1 serving.

*Chef's Tip*
Thermometers designed especially for a microwave oven are a useful accessory. Do not leave in the product while microwaving. Insert and read after food is removed from oven.

# *Barbecue Beef Sandwich*

Use leftover beef or buy cooked beef at the deli and have it thinly sliced.

**¼ cup chopped onion**
**2 teaspoons butter or margarine**

**2 teaspoons white wine vinegar**
**1 teaspoon Worcestershire sauce**
**1 teaspoon prepared mustard**
**1 tablespoon packed brown sugar**
**⅓ cup ketchup**
**6 ounces thinly sliced cooked roast beef**
**2 French rolls, cut in half lengthwise**

In a 1-quart microwave-safe dish, microwave onion and butter or margarine on 100% (HIGH) 1½ minutes. Remove from oven. Stir in vinegar, Worcestershire sauce, mustard, brown sugar and ketchup. Microwave on 100% (HIGH) 3 minutes, stirring once. Remove from oven. Stir in beef. Microwave on 100% (HIGH) 3 to 4 minutes or until beef is hot, stirring once. Spoon beef mixture onto bottom half of rolls. Replace top. Place each sandwich on a microwave-safe plate. Microwave each on 100% (HIGH) 30 seconds to 1 minute or until heated through. Makes 2 servings.

# Hot Seafood Salad Sandwich

A healthy light meal!

**2 ounces crab meat, flaked**
**1 tablespoon peeled chopped apple**
**1 teaspoon chopped green onion**
**1 tablespoon diced celery**
**1 teaspoon golden raisins**
**1 tablespoon mayonnaise**
**⅛ teaspoon curry powder**
**1 thick slice pumpernickel bread, toasted**

Place a paper towel in bottom of microwave oven. In a small bowl, combine crab, apple, green onion, celery, raisins, mayonnaise and curry powder. Mound on bread. Place sandwich on paper towel. Microwave on 100% (HIGH) 30 to 45 seconds or until heated through. Makes 1 serving.

# Pita-Pocket Ham Sandwiches

Armenian in origin, pita bread is available in white and whole-wheat in most supermarkets.

**1 tablespoon butter or margarine**
**½ small onion, thinly sliced**
**½ red or green bell pepper, thinly sliced**
**4 ounces fresh mushrooms, sliced**
**1 pita bread round, cut in half crosswise**
**Lettuce leaves**
**4 tomato slices**
**2 slices Swiss cheese**
**2 ounces thinly sliced ham**

In a microwave-safe casserole dish, place butter or margarine, onion, bell pepper and mushrooms. Cover tightly. Microwave on 100% (HIGH) 2 minutes; stir. Set aside. Place a paper towel in bottom of microwave oven. Place pita bread halves on paper towel. Microwave on 100% (HIGH) 5 seconds. Pull pita bread halves apart to form a pocket. Line pockets with lettuce leaves. Layer with tomato, cheese and ham. Spoon hot onion mixture into pockets. Makes 2 servings.

# Crunchy Egg Salad Sandwich

Chopped red pepper and alfalfa sprouts add crunch to this sandwich.

**1 egg**
**2 teaspoons mayonnaise**
**½ teaspoon Dijon-style mustard**
**2 teaspoons finely chopped red bell pepper**
**Salt**
**Pepper**
**1 slice pumpernickel bread**
**1 teaspoon butter or margarine**
**1 lettuce leaf**
**1 tablespoon alfalfa sprouts**

Lightly grease a custard cup. Break egg into cup. Pierce yolk with a fork. Cover tightly. Microwave on 50% (MEDIUM) 1 to 1½ minutes or until yolk is set. Let stand, covered, 3 minutes. Cool slightly. Chop egg finely. In a small bowl, combine egg, mayonnaise, mustard and bell pepper. Season to taste with salt and pepper. Set aside. Spread bread with butter or margarine. Place lettuce leaf on bread. Top with egg mixture. Sprinkle with sprouts. Makes 1 serving.

---

*Chef's Tip*
When in doubt as to time needed to microwave a food, always use less time. If needed, it's easy to add more cooking time.

---

# Tacos for Two

---

Beef is most tender when cooked to a medium-rare stage. Overcooking will toughen it.

> **8 ounces beef top round steak, cut in ¼-inch cubes**
> **1 small onion, cut in thin wedges**
> **1 large zucchini, diced**
> **½ cup prepared taco sauce**
> **½ teaspoon dried leaf oregano**
> **¼ teaspoon salt**
> **4 taco shells**
> **½ cup finely shredded lettuce**
> **½ cup (2-oz.) grated Cheddar cheese**
> **Hot-pepper sauce, if desired**

In a 1½ quart microwave-safe glass dish, combine beef, onion, zucchini, taco sauce, oregano and salt. Cover with wax paper. Microwave on 100% (HIGH) 3½ to 4 minutes or until beef is no longer pink, stirring once. Spoon into taco shells. Top with lettuce and cheese. Serve with hot-pepper sauce, if desired. Makes 2 servings.

# Green Chili Burrito

Add any fillings that come to mind for a personalized burrito.

⅓ cup spicy-flavored refried beans
1 (10-inch) flour tortilla
2 teaspoons finely chopped onion
2 tablespoons shredded Cheddar
  cheese
1 to 2 tablespoons green chili salsa

In a small microwave-safe bowl, microwave beans on 100% (HIGH) 45 seconds or until hot. Spread beans down center of tortilla to ¼-inch from edge. Sprinkle with onion and cheese; spoon on salsa. Fold sides of tortilla over filling to center. Fold bottom over filling and roll up, jelly-roll style, enclosing filling completely. Place on a microwave-safe serving plate. Microwave on 100% (HIGH) 1 to 1½ minutes or until heated through. Makes 1 serving.

# Quiche for One

This quiche cooks quicker and more evenly as the filling is preheated before being poured into the pie shell.

**1 recipe Pie Crust, page 309**
**1 egg**
**¼ cup milk or half and half**
**⅛ teaspoon salt**
**¼ cup (1-oz.) shredded Swiss cheese**
**6 thin slices zucchini**
**1 teaspoon finely chopped green**
   **onion**

Prepare Pie Crust as directed. Roll out and press into a 10-ounce microwave-safe quiche dish. Using a fork, prick bottom and sides several times. Microwave on 100% (HIGH) 1½ to 2 minutes or until just beginning to turn brown. Set aside. In a small microwave-safe bowl, beat egg, milk or half and half and salt. Microwave on 70% (MEDIUM-

HIGH) 1 minute or just until warm; stir. Set aside. Sprinkle cheese in bottom of prepared crust. Top with zucchini and green onion. Pour in egg mixture. Place an inverted saucer in microwave oven. Set dish on saucer. Microwave on 70% (MEDIUM-HIGH) 2½ to 3½ minutes or until center is just set. Let stand 3 minutes. Makes 1 serving.

# DESSERTS

Desserts! What wonders come to mind—the possibilities are endless in a microwave oven. Everything from Strawberry-Topped Cheesecake to Blueberry Cobbler. Desserts are enjoying great popularity and the fancier and gooier the better. One problem I find is that most dessert recipes serve four to six and what do you do with all the leftovers? This chapter includes many classics and lots of quick-to-fix yummy concoctions scaled down to one or two servings.

Chocolate melts great in a microwave oven; one ounce takes about one minute on 100% (HIGH). Always stir before adding more cooking time as chocolate usually holds its shape even though it is melted. Chocolate Marshmallow Fudge is one of my favorite sweets to microwave because I don't have to worry about it burning.

Fruit cooks very quickly and nicely in a microwave oven. If fruit needs to be peeled, like peaches or pears, microwave on 100%

(HIGH) thirty seconds per piece of fruit. The skin will slip off much easier. Reheating fruit desserts in a microwave oven, like Old-Fashioned Raisin Tarts, gives them that right-out-of-the-oven flavor. Warm store-bought chocolate-chip cookies on 100% (HIGH) ten to fifteen seconds for that just-baked taste.

Pie crusts can be successfully microwaved but will be pale compared to those baked conventionally. Pudding or fruit fillings can be microwaved and then poured into the cooked crust. Two-crust pies do not micro-wave well because the top crust traps steam and you end up with a soggy pie. Graham cracker-type crusts do very well in one min-ute on 100% (HIGH) to set the butter or margarine.

Cookware is never a problem for one or two serving-size recipes. Custard cups are perfect individual sizes. Invert and shape pie dough for tarts. Small (seven-inch) glass pie plates are ideal. Glass measures can be used to make puddings, pie fillings and sauces. Place a small drinking glass in the center of a one-quart casserole dish and it can double as a bundt pan.

Desserts are usually special and call for either an attractive presentation or a garnish. Paint the back of small fig leaves with melted chocolate, molding to form a cup. When set, remove fig leaves and fill with ice cream. Use Double Chocolate-Dipped Strawberries as a garnish or place three or four on a plate for an elegant dessert. I enjoy sharing my dessert recipes with you!

# Double Chocolate-Dipped Strawberries

Dip berries no more than three hours before serving as they tend to get soggy.

- **2 ounces semisweet chocolate**
- **2 teaspoons vegetable shortening**
- **6 large strawberries with stems, washed, well dried**
- **2 ounces white chocolate**

In a small microwave-safe dish, microwave semisweet chocolate and 1 teaspoon of shortening on 100% (HIGH) 1 minute or until completely melted; stir. Cool slightly. Holding berry by stem, dip ¾ of each berry into chocolate. Gently shake off excess chocolate. Place on wax paper. Refrigerate until cool and set. In a small microwave-safe dish, microwave white chocolate and remaining 1 teaspoon shortening on 100% (HIGH) 45 seconds or until completely melted; stir. Holding berry by stem, dip ½ of each berry in white chocolate. Place on wax paper to set. Use remaining chocolate as desired. Makes 2 servings.

# Chocolate Fondue

Who can resist making Chocolate Fondue for two.

> ½ cup whipping cream
> ¾ cup sugar
> 3 tablespoons butter or margarine
> 2 ounces unsweetened chocolate
> 5 large marshmallows
> ¼ teaspoon vanilla extract
> Dippers: banana slices, fresh strawberries, poundcake squares, vanilla wafers

In a 2-cup glass measure, combine cream, sugar, butter or margarine and chocolate. Microwave on 100% (HIGH) 3 to 4 minutes or until chocolate is completely melted, stirring 3 to 4 times. Stir in marshmallows until melted, then vanilla. Serve with assorted dippers. If needed, microwave fondue on 100% (HIGH) 30 seconds to reheat; stir. Makes about 1½ cups.

---

*Chef's Tip*
To melt chocolate squares, remove wrapper and place in a custard cup. Microwave on 100% (HIGH): 1 (1-oz.) square, 1- to 1½

minutes; 2 (1-oz.) squares, 2- to 2½ minutes. Stir once. Chocolate will still hold its shape even when melted. Stir before heating further.

# *Amaretto Pear*

The brighter color the pear skin, the prettier this dessert is. Red-skinned pears are best.

**2 tablespoons butter or margarine**
**1 tablespoon sugar**
**¼ teaspoon grated lemon peel**
**2 tablespoons Amaretto**
**1 large pear, cut in half lengthwise, cored**
**2 tablespoons sliced almonds, if desired**
**Fresh mint leaves**

In a small microwave-safe casserole dish, microwave butter or margarine on 100% (HIGH) 30 seconds or until melted. Remove from oven. Stir in sugar, lemon peel and Amaretto. Place pear halves, cut-side down, in dish. Sprinkle with almonds, if desired. Cover tightly. Microwave on 100% (HIGH) 3 to 3½ minutes or until pear is tender. Let stand, covered, 5 minutes. Place each pear half on a serving plate. Using a sharp paring knife, leave top intact and cut 6 lengthwise slits completely through pear. Gently separate slices, fanning out and laying at a 45-degree angle. Spoon sauce in cooking dish over pears. To garnish, place mint leaf at stem end. Makes 2 servings.

# Apricot Bars

Variations could include raspberry or strawberry jam.

- ½ **cup all-purpose flour**
- ⅓ **cup packed brown sugar**
- ½ **cup quick-cooking rolled oats**
- ¼ **cup butter or margarine, chopped**
- ⅓ **cup apricot jam**
- **1 tablespoon raisins**
- **1 tablespoon chopped walnuts**

In a small bowl, combine flour, brown sugar and oats. Using 2 knives or a pastry blender, cut in butter or margarine until mixture resembles coarse crumbs. Pat ⅔ of crumb mixture into a 4" × 3" microwave-safe casserole dish. Set aside. In a 1-cup glass measure, mix jam and raisins; spread over crumb mixture. Sprinkle with remaining ⅓ of crumb mixture, then nuts. Microwave on 70% (MEDIUM-HIGH) 5 to 6 minutes or until mixture is set and jam begins to bubble around edges. Cool to room temperature. Makes 6 bars.

# All-In-One-Pan Brownies

No mixing bowl to clean!

    ¼ **cup butter or margarine**
    1 **ounce unsweetened chocolate**
    ½ **cup sugar**
    ¼ **cup all-purpose flour**
    ½ **teaspoon vanilla extract**
    1 **egg, beaten**
    ½ **cup chopped nuts**
    ¼ **cup semisweet chocolate pieces**

In an 8″ × 4″ microwave-safe glass loaf pan, microwave butter or margarine and unsweetened chocolate on 100% (HIGH) 1 to 1½ minutes or until chocolate softens. Remove from oven. Stir in sugar and flour, then vanilla and egg. Blend well. Mix in nuts and chocolate pieces. Microwave on 70% (MEDIUM-HIGH) 2 to 4 minutes or until edges are just dry. Center may be slightly damp. Cool to room temperature. Makes 4 to 6 brownies.

# Crispy Butterscotch Bars

A grown-up version of a childhood favorite!

**3 tablespoons peanut butter**
**⅓ cup butterscotch pieces**
**1 cup crispy rice cereal**
**2 tablespoons semisweet chocolate pieces**

In a small microwave-safe bowl, microwave peanut butter and butterscotch pieces on 100% (HIGH) 30 seconds to 1 minute or until butterscotch pieces soften. Stir well. Quickly mix in rice cereal and chocolate pieces. Pour onto wax paper. Shape in a 6″ × 4″ rectangle. Cool to room temperature. Makes 4 bars.

# Chocolate Pudding Cake

This has its own chocolate pudding beneath a layer of cake. Garnish with ice cream or whipped cream.

¼ cup all-purpose flour
¼ cup plus 2 tablespoons sugar
1 tablespoon chopped walnuts
2 tablespoons unsweetened cocoa powder
½ teaspoon baking powder
½ cup plus 2 tablespoons water
1 tablespoon vegetable oil
¼ teaspoon vanilla extract

In a 1½ cup microwave-safe casserole dish, mix flour, ¼ cup of sugar, walnuts, 1 tablespoon of cocoa powder and baking powder. Stir in 2 tablespoons of water, oil and vanilla. Using back of a spoon, smooth batter. In a custard cup, combine remaining 1 tablespoon of cocoa powder and 2 tablespoons of sugar. Sprinkle over batter. In a 1-cup glass measure, microwave remaining ½ cup of water on 100% (HIGH) 1½ minutes or until boiling. Pour boiling water over batter. Microwave on 100% (HIGH) 1 minute. Rotate dish a half turn. Microwave on 100% (HIGH) 1½ to 2 minutes more or until cake is firm but still shiny on top. Makes 2 servings.

# Strawberry-Topped Cheesecakes

Try without strawberries; it tastes great plain, too.

> 1 recipe Graham Cracker Crust, page 309
> 1 (3-oz.) package cream cheese
> 3 tablespoons plus 2 teaspoons sugar
> ½ teaspoon vanilla extract
> ⅛ teaspoon grated lemon peel
> 1 egg
> 2 tablespoons dairy sour cream
> ½ cup sliced fresh strawberries or thawed frozen strawberries, chilled

Prepare crust as directed for tart shells. Set aside. In a small bowl, beat cream cheese, 3 tablespoons of sugar, ¼ teaspoon of vanilla, lemon peel and egg until fluffy. Pour into prepared tart shells. Microwave on 50% (MEDIUM) 2½ to 3 minutes or until center is almost set. To make topping, in a small custard cup, mix 2 teaspoons of sugar, ¼ teaspoon of vanilla and sour cream. Spoon evenly over cheesecakes. Microwave on 50% (MEDIUM) 30 seconds. Chill until ready to serve. To serve, top with berries. Makes 2 servings.

*Chef's Tip*
To soften cream cheese, remove wrapper from a 3-ounce package. Place in a small microwave-safe glass bowl and microwave on 30% (MEDIUM-LOW) 1 minute or until soft.

# Pink Strawberry Shortcake

A new twist to an old favorite.

**1 cup mashed fresh strawberries**
**3 tablespoons sugar**
**½ cup buttermilk baking mix**
**3 tablespoons water**
**6 large fresh strawberries, sliced**
**½ cup whipping cream, whipped, chilled**

In a small bowl, combine mashed strawberries and 2 tablespoons of sugar. Set aside. In a small bowl, combine remaining 1 tablespoon of sugar, baking mix, water and 3 tablespoons of sweetened mashed berries. Stir until mixture forms a dough and is pink in color throughout. Invert a microwave-safe flat-bottom casserole dish. Spoon dough in 2 equal mounds on bottom of dish. Form in rounds about 1-inch high. Microwave on 70% (MEDIUM-HIGH) 1½ to 2 minutes or until dry. Let stand 5 minutes. Split shortcakes horizontally. Place on 2 serving plates. Stir sliced berries into remaining sweetened mashed berries. Spoon ¼ of berries on each shortcake; replace tops. Top with remaining berries. Garnish with whipped cream. Makes 2 servings.

# Fruit-Filled Tarts

An elegant and luscious dessert for a special occasion.

**1 recipe Pie Crust, page 309**
**Water**
**Sugar**
**Sliced fruit such as strawberries,**

**kiwifruit, bananas or peaches,
  chilled
¼ cup currant jelly or marmalade**

Prepare Pie Crust as directed. Roll dough to a 9″ × 8″ rectangle. Cut 2 (4-inch) circles. Using a fork, prick entire surface of dough. Using a small cookie cutter or aspic cutters, cut enough designs from remaining dough to decorate edges of circles. Moisten outer edges of circles with water. Arrange designs, slightly overlapping, around edges. Using fingers, press down gently so designs adhere. Sprinkle with sugar. Cut 2 (6-inch) squares wax paper. Transfer tart shells to wax paper. Place in microwave oven. Microwave on 70% (**MEDIUM-HIGH**) 2 minutes or until shells start to dry. Using a pancake turner, remove to a wire rack; cool. Arrange fruit on shells. In a 1-cup glass measure, microwave jelly on 100% (**HIGH**) 30 seconds. Gently brush over fruit to cover. Makes 2 tarts.

# Old-Fashioned Raisin Tarts

I hope these bring back pleasant childhood memories!

**1 recipe Pie Crust, page 309**
**½ cup raisins**
**½ cup water**
**2 tablespoons packed brown sugar**
**1½ teaspoons cornstarch**
**Pinch ground cinnamon**

Prepare crust as directed for tart shells. Set aside. In a 2-cup glass measure, combine raisins and water. Microwave on 100% (HIGH) 3 minutes. Set aside. In a custard cup, combine brown sugar, cornstarch and cinnamon. Stir into raisin mixture. Microwave on 100% (HIGH) 3 to 4 minutes or until liquid is clear, stirring several times. Pour into prepared tart shells. Cool to room temperature. Makes 2 tarts.

# Graham Cracker Crust

Fill with your favorite pudding.

**1 tablespoon butter or margarine**
**⅓ cup graham cracker crumbs**
**Pinch ground cinnamon**

In a 1-cup glass measure, microwave butter or margarine, graham cracker crumbs and cinnamon on 100% (HIGH) 20 to 30 seconds or until butter or margarine melts. Stir to coat crumbs. Press crumbs on sides and bottom of a 6-inch pie plate or in 2 custard cups to form a crust. Microwave on 100% (HIGH) 30 seconds to set crust. Makes crust for 1 (6-inch) pie or 2 tart shells.

# Pie Crust

This recipe makes enough crust for one 6-inch pie, one small quiche or two tarts.

**½ cup all-purpose flour**
**2 tablespoons vegetable shortening**
**⅛ teaspoon salt**

## 1 tablespoon plus 1 teaspoon cold water

In a small bowl, combine flour, shortening and salt. Using a fork, blend until mixture is crumbly. Mix in 1 tablespoon of water. Stir or use hands to blend completely. Dough should hold together. If needed, add remaining 1 teaspoon water. When dough is smooth, shape in a ball, then flatten slightly. Roll on a floured surface or between 2 sheets wax paper. For 2 tart shells, roll in a 12″ × 6″ rectangle; cut in half. Shape to fit over 2 (6-oz.) inverted custard cups. Trim excess from edges. For a 6-inch pie plate, roll in a 9-inch circle. For a 10-ounce quiche dish, roll in a 9″ × 7″ rectangle. Gently lay dough in pan or dish. Press to fit. Crimp edges. Using a fork, prick bottom and sides several times. Microwave on 100% (HIGH) 1½ to 2 minutes or until just beginning to brown. Cool completely before filling. Makes crust for 1 (6-inch) pie, 1 (10-oz.) quiche or 2 tart shells.

## Variation
To make Chocolate Pie Crust, combine 1 tablespoon unsweetened cocoa powder and 2 tablespoons sugar with flour, shortening and salt.

# Blueberry Cobbler

Try substituting peaches or plums for blueberries.

**1 cup fresh blueberries**
**1 tablespoon quick-cooking tapioca**
**1 tablespoon sugar**
**½ teaspoon lemon juice**
**⅓ cup all-purpose flour**
**¼ teaspoon baking powder**
**1 tablespoon butter or margarine**
**⅛ teaspoon ground cinnamon**
**⅛ teaspoon grated lemon peel**
**2½ tablespoons milk**

In a 2-cup glass measure, mix berries, tapioca, sugar and lemon juice. Using a spoon, slightly crush berries to release some juice. Let stand 5 minutes. Microwave on 100% (HIGH) 3 to 4 minutes or until berry mixture comes to a boil, stirring once. Pour into a 1½ cup microwave-safe casserole dish. To make topping, in a small bowl, mix flour, baking powder, butter or margarine, cinnamon and lemon peel until crumbly. Add milk. Stir just until mixture holds together. Using a fork, break up topping in small pieces. Sprinkle over berry mixture. Microwave on 70% (MEDIUM-HIGH) 2 minutes or until topping appears dry but not hard. Serve warm. Makes 1 to 2 servings.

# *Chocolate Mousse*

Microwaved chocolate usually doesn't lose its shape when it melts. Stir to test.

- ¼ **cup semisweet chocolate pieces**
- ¼ **cup sugar**
- 1 **egg, lightly beaten**
- ¼ **teaspoon vanilla extract**
- ½ **cup whipping cream, whipped, chilled**

In a small microwave-safe bowl, microwave chocolate pieces on 100% (HIGH) 30 seconds or until melted. Stir until smooth. Stir in sugar, then egg and vanilla. Cool to room temperature. Fold in whipped cream. Spoon into 2 dessert dishes. Chill at least 1 hour. Makes 2 servings.

**Variation**
Stir 1 of following into melted chocolate mixture: 1 tablespoon Amaretto, 1 tablespoon Grand Marnier, 1 tablespoon peanut butter, ½ teaspoon instant coffee granules dissolved

in 1 tablespoon hot water, 1 tablespoon rum or 1 tablespoon chopped pecans.

---

*Chef's Tip*

To melt chocolate pieces, microwave in a small microwave-safe glass bowl on 100% (HIGH): ½ (6-oz.) package, 1- to 1½ minutes; 1 (6-oz.) package, 1½ to 2 minutes. Stir twice as chocolate pieces do not loose their shape when melted and can burn easily.

---

# Coconut Custard

---

Coconut adds lovely flavor as well as texture.

**¾ cup milk**
**1 egg, lightly beaten**
**1½ tablespoons sugar**
**½ teaspoon vanilla extract**
**2 tablespoons shredded unsweetened coconut**

In a 2-cup glass measure, microwave milk on 100% (HIGH) 2 minutes. Whisk in egg, sugar and vanilla. Sprinkle coconut into 2 custard cups. Pour milk mixture over coconut. Microwave on 50% (MEDIUM) 1½ minutes. Rotate cups a half turn. Microwave on 100% (HIGH) 1 to 1½ minutes more or until edges of custard are set. Let stand until center is set. Makes 2 servings.

# Chocolate Irish Cream

Strawberry ice cream is a good substitute for chocolate mint.

**¼ cup water**
**1½ teaspoons unflavored gelatin**
**¼ cup Irish cream liqueur**
**½ cup chocolate mint ice cream**
**2 tablespoons milk**
**Whipped cream**

In a 1-cup glass measure, microwave water on 100% (HIGH) 45 seconds or until boiling. Place gelatin in a blender. Pour in boiling water. Let stand 5 minutes or until gelatin softens. Process until gelatin dissolves. Add liqueur, ice cream and milk. Process until smooth. Pour into 2 wine glasses. Refrigerate 1 hour or until set. Garnish with whipped cream. Makes 2 servings.

# Lemon Mousse

This mousse is light in taste and low in calories —a refreshing dessert.

**4 tablespoons sugar**
**2 tablespoons cornstarch**
**¾ cup milk**
**½ teaspoon grated lemon peel**
**2 tablespoons lemon juice**
**1 egg white**
**½ cup sliced fresh strawberries, chilled**

In a 2-cup glass measure, combine 3 tablespoons of sugar and cornstarch. Gradually stir in milk. Microwave on 100% (HIGH) 1½ to 2 minutes or until mixture comes to a boil. Boil 30 seconds. Stir in lemon peel and juice. Cool to room temperature. In a small bowl, beat egg white until soft peaks form. Gradually beat in remaining 1 tablespoon of sugar. Fold into lemon mixture. Spoon into 2 serving dishes. Refrigerate 1 hour or until firm. To serve, top with berries. Makes 2 servings.

# Fresh Apple Tapioca

Served warm, this is a comforting snack or dessert.

1 large apple, peeled, cored,
  coarsely chopped
1 teaspoon lemon juice
1½ teaspoons quick-cooking tapioca
⅓ cup sugar
Pinch ground cinnamon

In a 1-quart microwave-safe dish, combine apple, lemon juice, tapioca, sugar and cinnamon. Cover tightly. Microwave on 100% (HIGH) 5 minutes or until apples are tender, stirring twice. Let stand 10 minutes; stir. Serve warm or cold. Makes 2 servings.

# Chocolate Marshmallow Fudge

Just enough fudge for two servings now and two later!

1 cup powdered sugar
3 tablespoons unsweetened cocoa
  powder

**3 tablespoons butter or margarine**
**1 tablespoon plus 1 teaspoon milk**
**⅓ cup miniature marshmallows**
**¼ teaspoon vanilla extract**
**¼ cup chopped walnuts**

In a small microwave-safe bowl, mix powdered sugar and cocoa powder. Add butter or margarine and milk. Microwave on 100% (HIGH) 1 minute or until butter or margarine melts. Remove from oven. Blend well. Stir in marshmallows. Microwave on 100% (HIGH) 15 seconds. Mix well. Stir in vanilla and nuts. Pour onto wax paper. Spread as thick as desired. Let stand until firm. If desired, refrigerate to speed setting process. Makes about ½ pound.

# *Peanut Brittle*

If only salted peanuts are available, rinse with water and dry on paper towels.

**½ cup light corn syrup**
**½ cup sugar**
**½ cup unsalted peanuts**
**1 tablespoon butter**
**½ teaspoon vanilla extract**
**½ teaspoon baking soda**

Grease a small baking sheet. In a 4-cup glass measure, mix corn syrup and sugar. Microwave on 100% (HIGH) 5 minutes, stirring several times. Remove from oven. Stir in peanuts and butter. Microwave on 100% (HIGH) 1 to 2 minutes or until golden brown. Stir in vanilla and baking soda. Quickly pour onto prepared baking sheet. Cool to room temperature. Break in pieces. Makes about ½ pound.

## Comparison to Metric Measure

| When You Know | Symbol | Multiply By | To Find | Symbol |
|---|---|---|---|---|
| teaspoons | tsp | 5.0 | milliliters | ml |
| tablespoons | tbsp | 15.0 | milliliters | ml |
| fluid ounces | fl. oz. | 30.0 | milliliters | ml |
| cups | c | 0.24 | liters | l |
| pints | pt. | 0.47 | liters | l |

| When You Know | Symbol | Multiply By | To Find | Symbol |
|---|---|---|---|---|
| quarts | qt. | 0.95 | liters | l |
| ounces | oz. | 28.0 | grams | g |
| pounds | lb. | 0.45 | kilograms | kg |
| Fahrenheit | F | ⁵/₉ (after subtracting 32) | Celsius | C |

319

# Liquid Measure to Liters

| | | |
|---|---|---|
| ¼ cup | = | 0.06 liters |
| ½ cup | = | 0.12 liters |
| ¾ cup | = | 0.18 liters |
| 1 cup | = | 0.24 liters |
| 1-¼ cups | = | 0.3  liters |
| 1½ cups | = | 0.36 liters |
| 2 cups | = | 0.48 liters |
| 2½ cups | = | 0.6  liters |
| 3 cups | = | 0.72 liters |
| 3½ cups | = | 0.84 liters |
| 4 cups | = | 0.96 liters |
| 4½ cups | = | 1.08 liters |
| 5 cups | = | 1.2  liters |
| 5½ cups | = | 1.32 liters |

# Liquid Measure to Milliliters

| | | |
|---|---|---|
| ¼ teaspoon | = | 1.25 milliliters |
| ½ teaspoon | = | 2.5  milliliters |
| ¾ teaspoon | = | 3.75 milliliters |
| 1 teaspoon | = | 5.0  milliliters |
| 1¼ teaspoons | = | 6.25 milliliters |
| 1½ teaspoons | = | 7.5  milliliters |
| 1¾ teaspoons | = | 8.75 milliliters |
| 2 teaspoons | = | 10.0  milliliters |
| 1 tablespoon | = | 15.0  milliliters |
| 2 tablespoons | = | 30.0  milliliters |

## POWER LEVEL SETTINGS

| Word Designation | Numerical Designation | Power Output at Setting | Percentage of HIGH Setting |
|---|---|---|---|
| HIGH | 10 | 650 watts | 100% |
| MEDIUM HIGH | 7 | 455 watts | 70% |
| MEDIUM | 5 | 325 watts | 50% |
| MEDIUM LOW | 3 | 195 watts | 30% |
| LOW | 1 | 65 watts | 10% |

# Fahrenheit to Celsius

| F | C |
|---|---|
| 200—205 | 95 |
| 220—225 | 105 |
| 245—250 | 120 |
| 275 | 135 |
| 300—305 | 150 |
| 325—330 | 165 |
| 345—350 | 175 |
| 370—375 | 190 |
| 400—405 | 205 |
| 425—430 | 220 |
| 445—450 | 230 |
| 470—475 | 245 |
| 500 | 260 |

The publishers hope that this
Large Print Book has brought
you pleasurable reading.
Each title is designed to make
the text as easy to see as possible.
G.K. Hall Large Print Books
are available from your library and
your local bookstore. Or, you can
receive information by mail on
upcoming and current Large Print Books
and order directly from the publishers.
Just send your name and address to:

G.K. Hall & Co.
70 Lincoln Street
Boston, Mass. 02111

or call, toll-free:

1-800-343-2806

*A note on the text*
Large print edition designed by
Michael S. Kelley
of G.K. Hall & Co.